Thyestes a tragedy, translated out of Seneca to which is added mock-thyestes, in burlesque / by F. W. Gent (1674)

J. W.

Thyestes a tragedy, translated out of Seneca to which is added mock-thyestes, in burlesque / by F. W. Gent

Thyestes.
Mock-Thyestes.
Seneca, Lucius Annaeus, ca. 4 B.C.-65 A.D.
J. W. fl. 1674.
Dedicatory signed : John Wright.
[16], 140, [2] p.
London : Printed by T. R. and N. T. for Allen Banks ..., 1674.
Woodward and McNaway / 1018
Wing / S2523
English
Reproduction of the original in the Bodleian Library

Early English Books Online (EEBO) Editions

Imagine holding history in your hands.

Now you can. Digitally preserved and previously accessible only through libraries as Early English Books Online, this rare material is now available in single print editions. Thousands of books written between 1475 and 1700 and ranging from religion to astronomy, medicine to music, can be delivered to your doorstep in individual volumes of high-quality historical reproductions.

We have been compiling these historic treasures for more than 70 years. Long before such a thing as "digital" even existed, ProQuest founder Eugene Power began the noble task of preserving the British Museum's collection on microfilm. He then sought out other rare and endangered titles, providing unparalleled access to these works and collaborating with the world's top academic institutions to make them widely available for the first time. This project furthers that original vision.

These texts have now made the full journey -- from their original printing-press versions available only in rare-book rooms to online library access to new single volumes made possible by the partnership between artifact preservation and modern printing technology. A portion of the proceeds from every book sold supports the libraries and institutions that made this collection possible, and that still work to preserve these invaluable treasures passed down through time.

This is history, traveling through time since the dawn of printing to your own personal library.

Initial Proquest EEBO Print Editions collections include:

Early Literature

This comprehensive collection begins with the famous Elizabethan Era that saw such literary giants as Chaucer, Shakespeare and Marlowe, as well as the introduction of the sonnet. Traveling through Jacobean and Restoration literature, the highlight of this series is the Pollard and Redgrave 1475-1640 selection of the rarest works from the English Renaissance.

Early Documents of World History

This collection combines early English perspectives on world history with documentation of Parliament records, royal decrees and military documents that reveal the delicate balance of Church and State in early English government. For social historians, almanacs and calendars offer insight into daily life of common citizens. This exhaustively complete series presents a thorough picture of history through the English Civil War.

Historical Almanacs

Historically, almanacs served a variety of purposes from the more practical, such as planting and harvesting crops and plotting nautical routes, to predicting the future through the movements of the stars. This collection provides a wide range of consecutive years of "almanacks" and calendars that depict a vast array of everyday life as it was several hundred years ago.

Early History of Astronomy & Space

Humankind has studied the skies for centuries, seeking to find our place in the universe. Some of the most important discoveries in the field of astronomy were made in these texts recorded by ancient stargazers, but almost as impactful were the perspectives of those who considered their discoveries to be heresy. Any independent astronomer will find this an invaluable collection of titles arguing the truth of the cosmic system.

Early History of Industry & Science

Acting as a kind of historical Wall Street, this collection of industry manuals and records explores the thriving industries of construction; textile, especially wool and linen; salt; livestock; and many more.

Early English Wit, Poetry & Satire

The power of literary device was never more in its prime than during this period of history, where a wide array of political and religious satire mocked the status quo and poetry called humankind to transcend the rigors of daily life through love, God or principle. This series comments on historical patterns of the human condition that are still visible today.

Early English Drama & Theatre

This collection needs no introduction, combining the works of some of the greatest canonical writers of all time, including many plays composed for royalty such as Queen Elizabeth I and King Edward VI. In addition, this series includes history and criticism of drama, as well as examinations of technique.

Early History of Travel & Geography

Offering a fascinating view into the perception of the world during the sixteenth and seventeenth centuries, this collection includes accounts of Columbus's discovery of the Americas and encompasses most of the Age of Discovery, during which Europeans and their descendants intensively explored and mapped the world. This series is a wealth of information from some the most groundbreaking explorers.

Early Fables & Fairy Tales

This series includes many translations, some illustrated, of some of the most well-known mythologies of today, including Aesop's Fables and English fairy tales, as well as many Greek, Latin and even Oriental parables and criticism and interpretation on the subject.

Early Documents of Language & Linguistics

The evolution of English and foreign languages is documented in these original texts studying and recording early philology from the study of a variety of languages including Greek, Latin and Chinese, as well as multilingual volumes, to current slang and obscure words. Translations from Latin, Hebrew and Aramaic, grammar treatises and even dictionaries and guides to translation make this collection rich in cultures from around the world.

Early History of the Law

With extensive collections of land tenure and business law "forms" in Great Britain, this is a comprehensive resource for all kinds of early English legal precedents from feudal to constitutional law, Jewish and Jesuit law, laws about public finance to food supply and forestry, and even "immoral conditions." An abundance of law dictionaries, philosophy and history and criticism completes this series.

Early History of Kings, Queens and Royalty

This collection includes debates on the divine right of kings, royal statutes and proclamations, and political ballads and songs as related to a number of English kings and queens, with notable concentrations on foreign rulers King Louis IX and King Louis XIV of France, and King Philip II of Spain. Writings on ancient rulers and royal tradition focus on Scottish and Roman kings, Cleopatra and the Biblical kings Nebuchadnezzar and Solomon.

Early History of Love, Marriage & Sex

Human relationships intrigued and baffled thinkers and writers well before the postmodern age of psychology and self-help. Now readers can access the insights and intricacies of Anglo-Saxon interactions in sex and love, marriage and politics, and the truth that lies somewhere in between action and thought.

Early History of Medicine, Health & Disease

This series includes fascinating studies on the human brain from as early as the 16th century, as well as early studies on the physiological effects of tobacco use. Anatomy texts, medical treatises and wound treatment are also discussed, revealing the exponential development of medical theory and practice over more than two hundred years.

Early History of Logic, Science and Math

The "hard sciences" developed exponentially during the 16th and 17th centuries, both relying upon centuries of tradition and adding to the foundation of modern application, as is evidenced by this extensive collection. This is a rich collection of practical mathematics as applied to business, carpentry and geography as well as explorations of mathematical instruments and arithmetic; logic and logicians such as Aristotle and Socrates; and a number of scientific disciplines from natural history to physics.

Early History of Military, War and Weaponry

Any professional or amateur student of war will thrill at the untold riches in this collection of war theory and practice in the early Western World. The Age of Discovery and Enlightenment was also a time of great political and religious unrest, revealed in accounts of conflicts such as the Wars of the Roses.

Early History of Food

This collection combines the commercial aspects of food handling, preservation and supply to the more specific aspects of canning and preserving, meat carving, brewing beer and even candy-making with fruits and flowers, with a large resource of cookery and recipe books. Not to be forgotten is a "the great eater of Kent," a study in food habits.

Early History of Religion

From the beginning of recorded history we have looked to the heavens for inspiration and guidance. In these early religious documents, sermons, and pamphlets, we see the spiritual impact on the lives of both royalty and the commoner. We also get insights into a clergy that was growing ever more powerful as a political force. This is one of the world's largest collections of religious works of this type, revealing much about our interpretation of the modern church and spirituality.

Early Social Customs

Social customs, human interaction and leisure are the driving force of any culture. These unique and quirky works give us a glimpse of interesting aspects of day-to-day life as it existed in an earlier time. With books on games, sports, traditions, festivals, and hobbies it is one of the most fascinating collections in the series.

old books. new life.

The BiblioLife Network

This project was made possible in part by the BiblioLife Network (BLN), a project aimed at addressing some of the huge challenges facing book preservationists around the world. The BLN includes libraries, library networks, archives, subject matter experts, online communities and library service providers. We believe every book ever published should be available as a high-quality print reproduction; printed on-demand anywhere in the world. This insures the ongoing accessibility of the content and helps generate sustainable revenue for the libraries and organizations that work to preserve these important materials.

The following book is in the "public domain" and represents an authentic reproduction of the text as printed by the original publisher. While we have attempted to accurately maintain the integrity of the original work, there are sometimes problems with the original work or the micro-film from which the books were digitized. This can result in minor errors in reproduction. Possible imperfections include missing and blurred pages, poor pictures, markings and other reproduction issues beyond our control. Because this work is culturally important, we have made it available as part of our commitment to protecting, preserving, and promoting the world's literature.

GUIDE TO FOLD-OUTS MAPS and OVERSIZED IMAGES

The book you are reading was digitized from microfilm captured over the past thirty to forty years. Years after the creation of the original microfilm, the book was converted to digital files and made available in an online database.

In an online database, page images do not need to conform to the size restrictions found in a printed book. When converting these images back into a printed bound book, the page sizes are standardized in ways that maintain the detail of the original. For large images, such as fold-out maps, the original page image is split into two or more pages

Guidelines used to determine how to split the page image follows:

• Some images are split vertically; large images require vertical and horizontal splits.
• For horizontal splits, the content is split left to right.
• For vertical splits, the content is split from top to bottom.
• For both vertical and horizontal splits, the image is processed from top left to bottom right.

THYESTES
A Tragedy,

Translated out of

SENECA:

To which is Added

MOCK-THYESTES,

IN

BURLESQUE.

By *J. W.* Gent.

——— *Miscentur seria Ludis.*

LONDON,
Printed by *T. R.* and *N. T.* for *Allen Banks,* at
St. Peter's Head in *White-Fryars,* 1674.

TO THE
Right Honourable,
Bennet LORD Sherard.

MY LORD,

A Part of Old Seneca presents it self by my Hand to your Lordships Patronage. I should justly blush at such a mean Return to your Lordships many Favours, had I not read how the Spanish Monarch, who Commands the Indies, accepts the Biscains Homage in the worthless Present of a few Maravidis; nor is the Gift ungrateful to him, since it speaks Subjection: In like manner my Lord, my only Ambition in this Dedication is to appear your Servant. I know your Lordships Goodness will pardon my Confident Address: 'Tis that Obleiging Nature, so radicated in the Sherards, that Commands the hearts of all men: 'Tis that which makes your Country truly Yours. And thus my Lord, you serve his Majesty both with your own and their Affections. Such is your

A 2   generous

[ ]

generous English *way of true endearment.* But *I must despair to speak your full worth in the narrow limits of a few Pages; Should I attempt to blazon your just value, it would extend this small Epistle to a Volume, and swell this little Volume to a Folio.* The *following Papers I submit to your free Censure; And if they prove so happy to attain any Degree in your Lordships favour, I shall despise the malice of all our little Critiques, who never exposing any thing of their own, (and so in no danger of Retaliation) make it their business to pique at every thing is published.* But *how e're this* Book *Succeeds, the Authors chief happiness is above their prejudice, which is, to be*

My Lord,
Your Lordships moſt Humble, and
moſt Obedient Servant,

John Wright.

ADVERTISEMENT.

Whether Seneca the Philosopher (to whose Pen some abscribe Three other Tragedy's) was the Original Author of this also, or some other Seneca, I know not: nor is it material; since Hensius esteems it Nulli cæterarum inferior. Let it suffice that the Author, *in many places,* appears much a Stoick, *and such was the* Philosopher. The following Translation was Writ many Years since, though Corrected, and rendred into something a more Fashionable Garb then it's first Dress, at

the

Advertisement.

the Intervals of a more profitable
Study *last long* Vacation. *And to a
few such Idle Hours must I attri-
bute the ensuing Farce, which way of
Pass-time was much more agreeable
to my Humor, then the continual
Glut of Ale and Tobacco, the ordina-
ry Entertainment of vacant time in
the Country.* I confess it is not now
very *Modish* to Translate *any thing
of this Nature from the* Latine,
when there are so many French
Play's *to be had, and those so well
Accepted.* Our Modern Drama-
tiques *present us with greater* Idæ-
a's *both of Vice and* Vertue: *Yet*
Ben: Johnson *thought a considera-
ble part of* Seneca's Thyestes *not
improper for the* English Stage *in
his time, when he took most of* Syl-
la's Ghost *from hence, and so well*

ap-

Advertisement.

approved of this way of Introduction, that he served himself of it
not only in his Tragedy of Cateline,
but also in his Devill's an Ass, a
Comedy, where he makes a Pug his
Home d'Intrigue   I know also
how much the Atreus and Thyestes
of Seneca hath been out-done by our
own Fletchers, Rollo, and Otto: Yet
I am confident the Comparison will
not be ungrateful to them that perceive, in many particulars the Drama of this Age to excell that of Seneca, as much as his was Improved
from the time when Thespis, who first
offer'd at Tragedy lead his Originall
of Actors about the Country in a Cart,
which served them both for a Con-
veyance and a Stage. So homely are
all Foundations, though of the fairest
Building.   Marginal Notes Expla-
nato-

Advertisement.

natory of the Poetique Fictions , I
have purposely omitted, as Imperti-
nent, knowing that most of those who
use this sort of Reading do either sufficiently understand, or despise those
little Misteries of Obsolete Poetry. For
those other few who still relish such
Chapon Bovilli , I only commend
'em to the next Dictionary, and that
will give 'em ample Satisfaction.
For a like Reason, I forbear to Pall
the Story with the thing call'd an
Argument, the No-Plot of these old
Tragedy's being sufficiently Intelligi-
ble, and so little needing a Clue, that
rather there wants more Labyrinth.

To

To my Worthy Friend, Mr. Jo. Wright, on his Translation of Thiestes, with the Travestie.

DId *Seneca* now live, himself would say
    That your Translation has not wrong'd
his *Play*;
But that in every Page, in every Line,
Your Language do's with equal splendor shine
His *Roman Habit*, and your *English Dress*
Themselves with a like Elegance express

                          Nor

r from your praise will it at all detract

To say the *Tragedy's* unfit to Act,

And that those *Playes* can never please the Age,

That hope for no Acquaintance with the Stage:

For to all those that judges are of Wit,

Fancy it self a *Theatre* will fit.

Each Scene expose to that Interior Eye,

And all th'e want of Actors too supply.

She can, without expence of Treasure raise

New Structures still to fit our several Playes,

For which but at the charges of a thought,

Nature's and Arts embellishments are bought

Her Scenes, tho' they exist but in the mind,

Are ever fram'd to what the Play design'd.

Nor is she forc'd by Scarcity to make

A trifling Buffoon the *Regalia* take :

Constraining none whom Nature has design'd,

Only to Ape a Fool, against his kind,

To

To mannage Scepters; left he should appear
With his ridiculous *Grimaces* where
Those loose Impertinences have no share.
Thus every Requisite is fitted so
That no dislike can from the Action grow:
And her *Ideal Theater* appears
With all the Lustre that attends on theirs.
Pleasant *Scarron*, whose *Mock-Æneas* made
Virgil himself smile at the *Masquerade*;
Too much beyond his power, did justly fear
Would *prove* the Works of our *Tragdian* here:
But what he fear'd may now your Glory prove
Whose *Quill* runs free where his durst never
    move :
And like the Sword that cur'd the wounds it
    gave,
Makes us such pleasure, so much laughter have,

After

[　]

After the *Passions* it had made us share!

That 'tis but Reason to maintain you are

Favour'd in *Verse* with *Ovid*'s happy *Muse*,

Whose Wit did with Success all *Subjects* use.

O: Salusbury.

The Authors Absence not permitting his Inspection, the Press hath suffered many Errors: of which the most Material are,

Page 5. line 4. deleatur period (.) p. 12. l. 4. read Sun. p. 18. l. 5. r. fortify. p. 20. l. 10. r. Let. p. 21. l. 17. r. vext p. 29. l. 6. r. Envoy p. 34. l. 6. r. doe p. 38. l. 2. r. with p. 41. l. 5, r. till it I left p. 50. l. 15. r. credit p. 51. l. 1. r. Brother p. 55. l. 15. r. Clotho p. 59. l. 3. r. yet p. 64. l. 8. r. vext p. 68. l. 6. r. No p. 69. l. 15. r. can tell p. 72. l. 17. r. Dews p. 73. l. 10. read No p. 74. l. 13. r. Belt p. 79. l. 1. r. Ho there p. 86. l. 9. r. Convex p. 89. l. ult. r. this p. 91. l. ult. r. gobets p. 93. l. 15. r. doth p. 96. l. 3. r. You'r vext l. 7. r. I Ignorant. p. 99. l. ult. Do then p. 110. l. 13. r. Cooks p. 105. l. 14. r. he. p. 110. l. 1. r. two p. 114. l. 7. r. Cuckoldry p. 126. l. 2. r. Creature p. 133. l. 9. r. Scribbellers p. 134. l. 1. r. Act 3. In the Epilogue l. 4. r. and as a Jest. l. 10. r. Farce.

Dramatis Personæ,

Tantalus's Ghost.

Megæra.

Atreus, King of *Argos.*

Thyestes, his Brother.

Plisthenes, his Son.

Two other Sons of *Thyestes, Mutes.*

A Servant, Attendant to *Atreus.*

Nuntius.

Chorus of Argives.

The Scene.

ARGOS:

PROLOGUE
To the Reader.

WIts, and Wit-Triers, who some Criticks Name
    Writers of Play's, and Dammers of the same,
Advance not farther then this Page; beware,
Since all that follows is Irregular.
For though this thing a Tragedy is stil'd,
'Tis free from Plot as any Sucking Child.
Nor Love, nor Honour here the Author show'd:
Nay, what is worse, no Bawd'ry A-la-mode.
No Amorous Song, nor a more Amorous Jigg,
Where Misses Coats twirl like a Whirlegig,
And such who next the Lamps themselves dispose,
Think thus to recompence the stink of those,
While she that Dances jilts the very eyes,
Allowing only these Discoveri's
A neat silk Leg, and pair of Holland Thighs.
Methinks I see some mighty Wit o'th Town
At this Express a most judicious frown,
And huff it thus (cocking his Caudubec)
S---What a Devil then must we expect?
Have patience, and I'le tell You what you shall
Meet here that's still in use Dramaticall.
High Lines, and Rime enough Sirs Ye shall have,
And Sentences most desperately Grave,
Dull Sence, and sometimes Huffs that Nature braves
And ('cause we cannot easily print a Dance)
A Farce i'th end out, A-la-mode-de-France.
                         THY.

A Tragedy,

Tranſlated out of

SENECA.

ACT. I.

TANTALUS. MEGÆRA.

Which of th' Infernal Powers doth
    thus compel

The wretched *Tantalus* to leave his Hell?

And, as a higher Damnation, ſhew again

That World where Bodies yet alive re-

  main?

Is ought found worſe than thirſty to abide

In Streams, and Hunger never ſatisfy'd?

Muſt I have *Siſyphus* his Stone, or feel

The giddy Torments of *Ixions* VVheel?

                        Or

Or fhall to me *Tytius* 's pains fucceed,

On whofe Immortal Liver Vultures feed:

For night repairing what was loft by day ,

He a frefh Monfter lies, and perfect Prey.

What Plague comes next? O thou who doft
  on thofe

That fuffer'd have the Old , New Pains
  impofe ,

Remorfelefs Judg of Souls who er'e you be,

Add if thou canft , add to my mifery.

Invent fuch horrid Torments that fhall make

Hells Porter fear , and the dark Regions
  quake.

Nay more my felf affright. Springing from
  me

Doth now arife a Monftrous Progeny.

Me their Progenitor they fhall out-act

In wickednefs, and guiltlefs make my fact

with

With Crimes unknown, and truly theirs.
　Each place
That's void in Hell, I'le furnish with my
　Race.
While our House stands, *Minos* shall have
　no need
Of other Clyents. ——
　Meg. Cursed Shade, proceed.
Their hated Bosoms with new fury fill.
And make them strive which shall surpass
　in Ill.
Let an alternate Rage their Souls inflame:
Such a blind Rage that knows nor Mean
　nor shame.
Let the first Root of wickedness in Thee
Grow to perfection in thy Progeny.
Nor let their Souls find leisure to repent
A past offence; but still new Crimes invent:
Doubling their Guilt under their Punish.
　ment.　　　　B 2　　　　Unsetled

Unfetled be their Throne, and short their
   Reign :

While giddy fortune gives them **Crowns** in
   vain.

Let her the Banish't raife toSoveraign place,

And Kings to the fame Banishment debafe,

With conftant trouble let their Kingdom
   burn,

And when the guilty Exiles fhall return ,

Let them afrefh to their old mifchiefs fall ,

As hateful to themfelves, as unto All,

Let **Rage** think nought unlawful to be done,

Let Brother, Brother fear; Mother the Son,

And Son the Mothers wrath.   Let Children dye

By wicked hands , others more wickedly

Be born. Let Wife her Husband kill, And
   may

They or'e the Seas their Enmity convey.

                     Let

Let effus'd bloud this and all Lands difdain,

Let conquering Luft over great Captains
    Reign

In their abhorred Courts. Let whoredom be

Counted no crime. Let hence Right, Amity,

And all accord of the fame bloud be gone.

And may their crimes reach Heaven; for
    when the Sun

Smiles on the world with an unclouded Ray

Let horrid Night ecclips the face of Day.

Fright hence their Houfhold-Gods weak
    Ayd; and fill

Their Place with Hate, death, murder,
    every Ill.

Be all this houfe with Garlands now array'd

And genial fires, to fpeak thy welcome,
    made.

Then let the Inhumanity of *Thrace*

Out-acted be on this more guilty Place.

Doth

Doth yet the Uncle Innocent remain?

Nor Father yet lament his Children flain?

When fhall their Limbs be from the Kitch-
    in ferv'd

Up to the Table, and in flices carv'd?

Let th' Uncles hearths blufh with his Ne-
    phews bloud:

Whiles feafts are made; Feafts furnifht
    with fuch food

As is no Novelty to Thee. Behold

This day is thine,here banquet uncontrould.

Now thy long fafting to the full requite.

Mingled with *Baccus* gift, this day, in fight

Of thee, fhall thine own blood be drunk. I
    now

Such dyet have invented as even thou,

Thou *Tantalus* woulft fly. Already? ftay;

Whether thus head-long doft thou force
    thy way?   *Tan.*

Tan. To the Infernal Lakes, and Streams
 that flip,

When I would drink, from my deluded
 Lip :

Back to the cheating Fruit I fly again,

Let me return to my old Place and pain.

Why am I ftay'd ? If I too happy feem ,

Gladly I'le change my banks : And to thy
 Stream

O *Phlegethon* let me be ever bound,

In waves of fire , while I both burn and
 dround.

Who er'e thou art that doft tormented lye

By the decree of fevere Deftiny :

Who er'e thou art, trembling and terrify'd

Under a ruinous Cave that doft abide,

Or fear'ft a falling Mountains ponderous
 fide.

VVho er'e thou art, whether thou feareſt more

The *Fury*'s Laſh, or hungry Lyons roar :

VVho er'e thou art who doſt, half burnt defend

Thy ſelf from flying brands, the Voice attend

Of *Tantalus* returning, credit me

VVho am experienc'd, Love your Miſery :

VVhen ſhall I fly the hated Light ?

　Meg. Engage

Thou firſt this houſe in diſcord, and wars Rage :

VVar, ſo much lov'd of Kings in every Age.

Thus fire their Salvage breaſts. ———

　Tan. Fates angry doom

I'de ſuffer not inflict : behold I come

　　　　　　　　　　Like

Like a dire-Vapour that has cleft the
  Ground,

Or a sad Pestilence dispersing round

Infection through th'affrighted world, ——
  Must I

To such black Crimes my Nephews hearts
  apply?

Great King and Parent of the Deities,

And Ours, although it shames thee, Ours
  likewise;

My Tongue will not forbear her Office,
  though

She double Torments for it undergo ——

Your hands and Altars with such damn'd
  Offence

Profane not: here I'le stand, and guard it
  hence. ——

VVhy

VVhy fright'ft thou me with threatned
 blows ? what makes

Thee menace thus with thy contorted
 Snakes ?

VVhy doft increafe my hunger? Oh my
 heart

Burns with new Thirft : Fire feeds on every part.

I follow thee.

  Meg. Seeds of Revenge and hate

Sow in this houfe. Let this, this be their
 fate,

That imitating thee their Sire they, now

May thirft each others blood as water thou.

The houfe thy prefence feels; behold, no
 lefs

Then the whole Fabrique fhakes at thy
 accefs.

        'Tis

'Tis acted to the full. Now sink to Hell

Thy proper Place , and Rivers known too
well :

Earth's burthen'd with thy weight. Dost
not perceive

The Springs shrink inward, and their Foun-
tains leave

The wind, 'gainst nature hot, few Clouds
doth bear

Trees blasted at thy sight, naked appear,

Their fruit and leaves fall'n off. Two
Neighbouring Seas

This *Isthmos* doth divide , seest thou how
these

At thy sight ebbing do augment their shore,

And at a new unusual distance Roar.

Lerna shrinks back, *Inachus* in full speed

Sees thee , and stops his Course: nor doth
proceed *Alphaus*

Alpheus sacred wave. *Citheron's* head
Is white no more, his snowy *Peruque* fled.
Such Thirst as *Argos* underwent of old
Is fear'd again. The Son himself, behold,
Doubts to go on and mend the faintin
  Light,
Or the world bury in perpetual Night.

Chorus, Of *Argives.*

If any of the Powers Above
Doth still *Achaian Argo's* love,
Pisa's aspiring Turrets, and
The Kingdoms of this neck of Land;
If our Twin-Ports and sever'd Seas
Do any blest Immortal please:
Or tall *Taygetus* (whose Snows
Congeal to Ice when *Boreas* blows,

Bu

But thaw again when milder weather

Brings the rich Eastern Traffique hither.

At whose foot clear *Alphaus* flows

Renoun'd for the *Olympick* shows :

Hear us propitious Heaven, and bless

Us from Alternate-wickedness ;

Let not the Nephews greater be

Then Grandsire in Impiety :

Nor this succeeding Age invent

Crimes which the former never meant.

May now at length the Progeny

Of thirsty *Tantalus* agree,

As weary'd into Peace again:

Discord hath had too long a Reign,

Guilt nought avails, nor Innocence;

Both alike punisht as Offence.

Such

Such faith as to his Lord he bare

False * *Myrtilus* found from his Heir,

* *Myrtilus* Charioteer to *Oenomaus* King of *Argos*, was by *Pelops* corrupted to betray his Masters Life in a Chariot-Race. By this means *Pelops* not only won the Race, but his Mistress, whom *Oenomaus* her Father had appointed the fair Prize of such a Conquest: But *Pelops*, now his Son in Law and Successor, allow'd the Treacherous *Myrtilus* no other Reward then to be cast into the Neighbouring Sea, from thence called *Mare Myrtoum.*

Waves gave him death, and to the same

He in Exchange did give his Name.

No story better known then this

To the *Ionian* Sayler is.

Thy Infant-Son met death, while he

Did run to meet a kiss from thee;

Inhumane Parent; *Tantalus*,

Too immaturely falling thus

A Sacrifice; each part of him

Thy hand cut out, and cook'd each Limb;

To

To make a cursed Feast of these
For the abhorring Deity's.
Hunger they gave for this Repast,
And thirst that shall for ever last:
Nor could a fitter Pain have been
For the Offender or the Sin.
Deluded *Tantalus* remains
Still vext with Hungers innate Pains;
Rich-laden boughs hang neer his sight,
Swifter then Birds of strongest flight;
These stoop to meet his Lips, but then
Mock his stretch't Jaws, and rise again,
Often abus'd with this deceit,
He now neglects the tempting Cheat:
And though impatient of delay,
Turns his sad eye another way,
And shuts his empty mouth again
Confining there fierce hungers pain.

Her

Her Wealth the Tree then lower bends;

And the insulting Fruit descends,

At this his Appetite revives;

But when once more he vainly strives

To reach the boughs, once more they rise;

And all the Autumn upward fly's.

Now Thirst, great as his hunger is,

Succeeds; when his Veins burn with this

He Courts the passing VVaves while they

Are by their Current forc'd away.

Their empty Channel these forsake,

And him that strives to overtake:

VVho snatching at the flying Floud

In greedy haste drinks sand and Mud.

ACT

ACT. II.

Atreus, a Servant.

DUll Coward that I am! fenceleſs! (and what

I count in Majeſty the greateſt Blot)

O unreveng'd! Do I, when Crimes ſo great

Are by a Brother acted, ſuch Deceit,

Such breach of Juſtice, poorly thus in vain

My Anger ſpeak? and nothing but com-
plain?

All *Argos* now in Arms ſhould own my ſide,

And my proud Navy on theſe Twin-Seas
Ride.

Country and Town ſhould with my fire-
ings ſhine,

And brighter then thoſe flames this ſword
of mine.   C   Then

Then let this Land groan with our Ca-
  valry ;
Let not our Foe in the Woods sculking
  lye,
Nor on the Hills securely fortifie.

Empty be *Argos* wals, in numerous swarms,
VVhile all her People cry to Arms, to
  Arms.
VVho hides his head, thinking it so to save,
May he for ever hide it in the Grave.
Let Renown'd *Pelops* House upon me fall,
So it my Brothers Ruine prove withall.
Courage my Soul! something thou now
  must act,
All Ages shall report, none praise the fact:
A Crime that so transendant wicked is,
My Brother shall in Envy wish it his.

His

His Vilany is not reveng'd unless

Out-done : But what can pass his wickednefs ?

Doth Exile humble him ? did ever he

Embrace a Mean when in Profperity,

Or reft content when low ? I him for one

Not to be tamed, fufficiently have known :

Broke he may be, not bent. Affault him
then

Before he thee affaults, or leavy's men ;

Kill or be kill'd : this offer'd is alike

To both, but hee's moft fafe who firft
fhall ftrike.

    Ser. Fear you not, Sir, the Peoples

Tongues ? *Air.* Not I :

For this I count a Kings chief Royalty,

That his bad Actions, all his Subjects are

By Fear compell'd as well to praife, as bear.

Ser. Such who by Fear are Loyal made, ev'n thofe

Forc'd by that fear do firft become your Foes;

But if you would true Glory, Sir, attain,

You o're the heart, and not the Tongue muft Reign.

Atr. Falfe Glory have the Great, the Vulgar true.

Let 'em diflike it, fo my Will they do.

Ser. Let Kings Command what's honeft, and they muft.

Atr. Such Kings who only may command what's juft

Rule by precarious Power. *Ser.* Yet needs muft be

That Throne unfetled, where's nor Piety,

Nor

Nor fhame of VVrong, nor care of Right,
nor Faith.

   Atr. Thefe private Virtues are. A
Crown who hath

Should know no Law but his own Royal
will.

   Ser. Can you be guiltlefs and a Brother
kill.

   Atr. What's on a Brother Villany to act,
On him but Jufticeis. What hellifh Fact

Hath henot try'd? what fcapes him? he
his own

By VVhoredom made my VVife, by Theft
my Throne.

By fuch bafe frauds he gain'd the Antient
Signe

Of Soveraign Power, and next this houfe of
mine.

A

A well-known fhy-kept Ram , fam'd *Pelops* Fold

Did, his rich Flocks far richer Leader, hold,

A fleece he not of VVool but Gold doth
    wear ,

Scepters of which our new Kings ufe to
    bear ;

Who hath this hath the Crown: with it
    the fate

Of our houfe goes along infeperate.   (high

Safe fed this facred Beaft in Meads , which

Fences of ftone enclofe and fortifie.

This bold attempting Trayter, having made

My VVife a Party , hence that beaft con-
    vey'd.

From this fprings all our mutual ftrife.
    Now goes

He through my Kingdoms, and Sedition
    fowes,   VVhere's

Where's he not guilty? he corrupted hath

My Wife, ruin'd my house, and broke his
   faith;

My Iffue's doubtful, nothing fure but this,

That my worft Enemy my Brother is.

VVhy ftopft thou *Atreus?* on at length begin

Thy brave Revenge: Courage; mind what
   has been

By *Tantalus* and *Pelops* done; thine Eye

And hand within unto their Deeds apply.

Then fay what courfe in my Revenge is beft?

   Ser. Let your juft fword, Sir, pierce
his guilty breaft.

   Atr. Mild Kings do only kill; You
of the end

Of torment fpeak, I torment do intend.

Aſſued-for favour in my Reign ſhall be
Bare death eſteem'd. . *Ser.* Moves you no
   piety ?

    Atr. Hence thou vain ſhadow, *Piety*, if
thou

VVaſt ever here? hence, I abjure thee now.
Ye Furies, Hells black Miſſionaries, let
Me begg your ayd to make my Rage com-
   pleat.

Bring here two brands of your Infernal fire;
And in this breaſt a doubl●ate inſpire.

    Ser. VVhat frenzie drives you thus
to unknown Deeds ?

    Atr. Such as the common mean of
Grief exceeds.

I'de uſe the worſt of Cruelties, but fear
They'd all too ſlight and innocent appear.

                      Ser.

Ser. The Sword? *At.* A trifle. *Ser.*
Fire? *At.* A trifle ftill.

    Ser. VVhat Inftrument fhall your Re-
venge fulfill.

    Atr. Thyeftes felf. *Ser.* And wrath it
felf has lefs

Of Plague then him. *Atr.* Horror, I muft
  confefs,

Invades my trembling Soul? I'me forc'd.
  but know

Not whether yet I'me forc'd, and on muft
  go. ——

    Here *Tantalus* and *Megera* are fuppofed to pafs over
the Stage.

The Center groans; the Heavens in Thunder fpeak;

And all my houfe cracks as the Roof would
break:

                  The

The Lares turn their looks ; be done , be
   done

This Crime , whofe fight the fearful Gods
   do fhun.

   Ser. What, Royal Sir, do you at length
defign ?

   Atr. I know not what great Act, beyond
the Line

Of humane Cuftome , more then ufual
   fwells

My Soul, and forward my flow hand com-
   pells :

What 'tis I know not ; fomething great
   it is ———

                   [Paufes a while]

Thus let it be; my Soul, refolve on this;

                                     A

A fit Deed for *Thyeftes*, and for me.

Let us both act. —— Th' * *Odryfian* houfe did fee

The Story of *Tereus* King of *Thrace.* See the Meta-morphofis, Lib. 6.

Inhumane feafts. I grant, the Crime, though high,

Yet hath been done already; fomething I

Would have as new, as bad, *Progne*! Infpire,

Thou cruel Parent, in my breaft the fire

Of thy Revenge. Our caufe is Parrallel.

Affift me ; and to act my hands compell.

Let the pleas'd Father on his Children feed,

And carve their Limbs. I this, I like indeed,

Tis well; exceeding well. But ich' mean time

Where's he? And I, why fo long free from Crime ?

Me

Methinks I see the Tragick Scene; and how
He eats himself no Father, even now.———

Heart! dost thou faint, before thou hast be-
gun

The Generous Act? It must, it shall be done.
On then; since he in his own person shall
Commit the highest Villany of all.

Ser. But by what Wiles can we er'e
bring him here,

Whose caution renders him so full of fear?

At. I le bate, then take him, with his
own Desires.

He hopes my Crowns; and while he thus
aspires

He'd meet a flaming Thunderbolt, for them
The Adriatique Gulf he would contemn;
And pass the Libyck shelves; nay more he
will

(Which he esteems of all the greatest Ill)

For

For them his Brother fee. *Ser.* Yet who
    fhall give

The pledg of Peace? or who will he believe?
       Atr. Vain hope is credulous. My
    Sons fhall bear

From me this envy to their Uncles ear,

And fue in wining terms, that he would
    leave

His Exile for a Pallace, and receive

A Crown with half my Kingdom. Should
    he prove

Obdurate like himfelf; yet this would move

His children; who in thefe affairs untaught

And tyred with miferies, are eafily caught,

And they'l prevail with him. Love of Rule
    here,

His antient frenzie; grief and trouble there,

            Though

Though ne're so obstinate will conquer
him.

   Ser. Time now hath made his sorrows'
light to seem.

   Atr. Time doth augment our miseries,
not cure:

They'r light to suffer, heavy to endure.

   Ser. Yet find some other Messengers
for this:

Youth to ill counsell prone and docile is.

They may by him to act 'gainst you be led.

Mischief oft falls on the Contrivers head.

   Atr. No other Tutor than Ambition
needs,   (Deeds.

To teach 'em fraud and such Nefarious,

Dost doubt they'l not be wicked made ?

they be   (elty,

So born. And what you think dire Cru-

Is now, perhaps, by him designed on me.

                             Ser.

Ser. Should your Sons know the Plot,
their Childhood may
(Unapt for secrecy) the same betray.

Atr. Silence I've learnt from sorrows
not a few.

Ser. Must they be strangers then to
what they do?

Atr. Yes: Be they guiltless still. I
see no need
To make my Sons my Partners in the
Deed.
We our Revenge will act alone— My mind
Thou now dost shrink from what was first
design'd:
Spare them, spare him: Let *Agamemnon* be
And *Menelaus* of my Privicie
In this Affair. Of their Original,
Doubtful as yet, the truth thus find I shall.

If they to act their parts unwilling seem,
And grieve at our Diffention, calling him
Their Uncle, he their Father is. —— Well
　go
They shall : but about what they must not
　know:
Their dubious face will what's within
　reveal :
Therefore from them, and all elfe, this
　conceal.

　　Ser. Sir, I conceive this needs not, Faith
　and fear,
But chiefly Faith will clofely keep it here.

Chorus.

At length the happy time occurs
That reconciles the Succeffors

Of

Of Royal *Inachus.* What made
Ye thus each others Life invade,
Unkindly equal Brothers, why
Sought ye a Crown in such Impiety?
Greatnefs ye do not rightly prize;
Nor know in what a Kingdom lyes.
Riches cannot inaugurate
A King, nor *Tyrian* Robes of State,
Nor Diadems, nor Roofs that may
With Golden frets out-fhine the day;
He is a King whofe mind is free
From every Paffions tyranny;
Whom, nor th'inconftant Vulgars praife,
Nor impotent Ambition, fways.
Such is the man whofe richer breaft
Contemns the Treafures of the Weft;
Tagus bright Sands, he doth defpife,
And *Lybia's* wealthy Graneries.

Whofe

Whose Soul no terror feels when *Jove*
Dischargeth Lightning from above.
Or when the *Adriatique* waves
Swell to the Clouds, and *Eurus* raves,
His great heart shakes or shrinks no more
Then doth the Neighbouring Rocks or
    shore.
Whose Noble soul, nor sword, nor spear
Can subject to unmanly fear.
He plac'd in a secure Estate,
Looks down on all those sports of Fate,
Grandure and Triumphs, and sees there,
How much below his thoughts they are.
Nor will he murmur at his End,
But meet pale death and call him friend.
None of those Kings can him infest,
The scatter'd *Daca* who molest;

Or

Or who by that Red Sea abide
With Pearls enrich'd and beautifi'd ;
Him the *Armenian* cannot harm ,
Who so confides in his own Arm ,
He slites th' advantage of his hills;
Nor *German* , who when winter chills
Other mens veins, sports on the Ice ;
Nor *Seres* clad in silks of price.
His Kingdom is within : No force
He needs to keep his Crown, of Horse;
No need of Swords, or shafts whereby
The *Parthians* Conquer when they fly ;
No need of the *Balista's* ayde
The walls with Battery to Invade.
VVho fears not is a King. And he
That will, may have this Royaltie.
While he that loves Ambitions pains,
On the Courts slippery top remains ;

Let

Let me sweet Peace enjoy : content
I am to live where none frequent :
There shall I fill my longing breast
VVith the still blessings of soft Rest,
Free from their Knowledg great who are,
Free from the noise of business, there
I'le cast my Life, and thus shall I
Rich in an humble fortune dye.
But heavy doth that death befall
To him, who too much known to all
By fame of his great honours past,
Dyes to himself unknown at last.

ACT.

ACT III.

Enter *Thyestes, Plisthenes*, **and his Two other Sons.**

My Countrys long'd for fight I now pof-
   fefs ;

The greateft good that can fad Exiles blefs.

My Native Soil, and Country-gods I fee;

(If Gods they are who fo neglected me;)

I fee the towrs the *Cyclops* work that are,

No Mortal can raife ftructures half fo fair.

Oft with applaufe have I at that fam'd
   place ·

In *Pelops* Royal Chariot won the Race.

Me the whole Town will meet returning
   home ;

Nay *Atreus* too, whofe fight I hate, will
   come.   D 3   Then

Then let me back again to woods obscure,

And wish the Beasts a life like theirs endure.

A Crowns false splendor shall not me en-
flame:

Mind not the Gift, but him that gives the
same.

Chearful I was when in a low Estate :

Now I from Exile am recall'd, and Fate

Doth smile, I'me sad.   Something within
doth cry,

Turn back again: I move unwillingly.

      Plisthenes (aside.)

VVhat means my Father thus his pace
to slack ?

He seems much unresolv'd , and oft looks
back.

        Thy.

Thy. Why do I waver thus? why do I strain

My wits, and dwell on that which is so plain?

Shall I Two such uncertain things as are

My Brother, and a Kingdom trust? and fear

Those Ills which time doth now familiar make?

And my commodious sufferings forsake?

My former Life, though wretched, pleaseth me:

Then let me back retire, while yet I'me free.

 Plist. Dear Sir, why turn you from your Countrys sight?   (flights

and why such Royal Presents do you

our Brothers wrath is ended, he to you

ffers a Peace, and half his Kingdom too.

YOu to your felf he will reftore.   *Thy.* A

   kind   (mind.

Of ftrange and unknown Terror chills my

No caufe I have, yet fear. I much defire

Forward to go, yet forc'd am to retire.

So have I feen a raging ftorm prevail

Againft a fhip ; fpight of her Oar and Sail.

    Plift, Contemn fuch idle fears, think

how at your   (dure.

Courted Return you'l have a Kings Gran-

   Thy. That, (having power of my own

Life, I've got.

    Pl ft. Power's the chief thing.   *Thy.*

Nothing if valued not.

   Plift. It may defcend to us. *Thy.* Two

cannot fway

    One Scepter——

Plift.——Who'd not happy be that may ?

                         Thy.

Thy- Believe me Greatnefs is an empty
Name:

And hard Fate's vainly fear'd. Since firſt I
came

Unto a Throne, till it left , I nef'e

Was free , but even mine own Guards did
fear.

How ſweet it is, to live from ſtrife ſecure,

To feed on Diſhes wholſom though but
poor !

The humble Cottage knows not villany,

And ſlender dyet is from Poyſon free :

That's drunk in Plate. With good expe-
rience I

Approve the low eſtate above the high.

* I own no Castles that on hills do stand,

And from that height the neigbouring
    Towns command :

* Here *Seneca* by a kind of Antecronism, taxeth the *Romans* in his Age, in their Buildings, Feasts, Baths, &c. of which particulars see at large, *Seneca*'s Epistles 122.

No Ivory frets adorn my roof : and when

I sleep I'me guarded by no Halbert-men ;

With no whole fleet I fish: No Rampiers I

Build to prescribe the Sea: Nor banquet by

The Lands Oppression : Nor beyond the
    Gete

Or *Parthian* have I Lands as rich as great :

I'me not adord 'stead of neglected *Jove*:

Nor doth my Pallace roof support a Grove:

I have no Baths like Seas: nor do I choose

The day for sleep , the night for drinking
    use.

Yet

Yet in my abject fortune am secure

Without a guard, and fearless being poor;

In it I meet content, and to have this

Without a Kingdom, the best Kingdom is.

Plist. But when the gods to us a Crown commit

commit

We should not slight the Gift——

Thy.—————— Nor covet it.

Plist. That you would Reign your Bro-

rher doth desire.

Thy. Doth he? that raiseth my su-

spition higher.

Plist. True Piety from whence she fled

doth use

Back to return, and her lost strength re-

news.   (will

Th. Atreus his Brother love? first *Arctos*

Set in the waves; *Sicilian* Seas be still;

In

In the _Ionian_ Ocean Corn will grow ;

Darkneſs will ſhine, before he will do ſo:

Firſt fire with water, wind with waves, and
　Life

With death , will enter League, and end
　their ſtrife.

　　Pliſt. What fraud ſuſpect you? _Thy._ All,
Nor can I ſee

VVhat not to doubt from ſuch an Enemy.

　　Pliſt. How can his Pow'r hurt you? _Thy._
Me? I deſpiſe

His Rage: Ye only cauſe my jealouſies.

　　　Pliſt. Fear you deceit when in the
　Trap? we are

Cautious too late when taken in the ſnare

Then let us on.————

　　　Thy. ————Witneſs ye gods to this?
I follow them, I lead 'em not amiſs.

　　　　　　　　　　　　Pliſt.

Pli∫t. Fearle∫s let us proceed. Pro∫per

th' event   (tent.

Kind Heaven, let it be good as is th' In+

Enter *Atreus*, Attended.

Atr. At length the Game which I ∫o

long have ∫aught,   (*a∫ide*)

VVith all his Breed, in my ∫pread Toils is

caught.

I have him now; and with him my de∫ire.

Behold *Thye∫tes* comes, he comes intire.

My or'e-joyd ∫oul will temper ∫carce admit,

Nor my unbroke fierce Pa∫∫ion know the

Bit;

So when the *Vmbrian* Lime-hound through

the field

Hunts on a Trayl; and in a Lea∫h is held;

VVhil∫t he perceives the Game far off to be

Silent and ∫tanch on the dead Scent runs he:

But

But when the Quarry's nigh, his gesture
   speaks

The welcome News; stiff doth he draw,
   and breaks

From his slow Master's hand. Rage never
   cou'd

Take a Disguize when once her ayme was
   blood;

Yet mine shall.——Look: do but observe
   him there

How his wild superfluities of Hair

Hang rudely or'e his sad dejected Eyes:

His Beard too, how undecently it lyes.

              [goes to *Thyestes.*

Brother, i've past my Faith: doubt me
   no more.

Your dearest sight doth my lost joyes restore.

                            Blcs

Bless me with your so coveted Embrace.

Henceforth, all Enmity let us displace

From our abused breasts; and entertain

The Piety of Brothers once again.

Thy. Your Goodness, Sir, is of such force,
 I can't

Frame an Excuse; but all my fault must
 grant.

Your Goodness makes me worse appear
 one who   (too

Have wrong'd a Brother, and a Brother

So eminent for generous Love as you.

[Kneels,

who ner'e did, do weeping, you implore

And with these hands that never beg'd before   (please

Thus humbly supplicate that you would

To pardon all; and for my faith take these,

These Infant Hostages: ——————   *Atr.*

Atr. — — Rise from my feet,
And as a Brother my Embraces meet,

            [To the Children.

Kiss me sweet Innocents, esteem'd aright
Both a support to Parents, and Delight

               [to *Thyestes*.

Off with these Rags, wound not my pitty-
   ing Eye
VVith the sad object of your Poverty,
And Robes assume like mine. More praise I
   gain
To give you half, then a sole Monarch
   Reign;
Therefore take half my Realm. A Crown
   to find
Speaks Chance, but to bestow the bravest
   Mind.

                       Thy.

Thy. Dear Brother, may the bounteous gods above

Return a blessing great as is your Love.

But my deformed head no Crown will wear;

Nor this unhappy hand a Scepter bear.

A poor *Plebeian* let me still remain. ————

     Atr. Not so: this Land may well two Kings contein.

     Thy. VVhat's yours I mine esteem: Brother, take all.

     Atr. VVho'd slight the favours that from Fortune fall?

     Thy. VVho'd not that knows how slippery they are?

     Atr. Of so great Glory will ye me debarre?

                     H   *Thy.*

Thy. Your Glory Sir, you have already won,

But mine remains, which is such Gifts to shun.

Atr. No more Excuse, I beg. Unless you own

Part of the Goverment, I will have none.

Thy. Well, I accept. Henceforth the Name be mine;

But I my self with all the Power thine.

Atr. VVear then your Crown: while I, without delay

Th' intended Sacrifice to Heaven pay.

Chorus.

Who'ld Credit this? *Atreus,* of late
So cruel, and so obstinate,

VVhen

VV hen he his suppliant brother spyed,

Conscious of Gilt, stood stupify'd.

Oh Love; what Power can thine excell ?

Discord with strangers long may dwell,

But where the Tyes of blood and thee

Conjoyn, short is that Enmity.

Private Affronts, though urg'd too far,

Rais'd a Revenge in Publick war.

While new-rais'd Troops the Country
  fright,

And Swords impatient for a fight :

Now finding what so long they'd sought,

Look bright and chearful with the thought.

Fraternal Piety takes place,

Forcing the Brothers to embrace,

Which of your Powers , kind Heaven, to
  cease

Hath caused such war in such a Peace ?

VVhen

VVhen Civil, the worſt ſort of Foes,

Did all *Mycene* diſcompoſe ;

The Mother fear'd her Infants Life ;

Her armed Husbands loſs, the VVife.

The conquering Sword , when firſt they

   drew,

Orecome with peacefull Ruſt they view.

Some dreſs their Arms : ſome buſy were

The Forts half ruin'd, to repair :

Some had Commiſſion to ſurvey

The Wall, and make up the Decay.

By ſome the Gates were ſtrongly bar'd ;

Others by Night maintain the Guard.

The empty Name of VVar doth bring

More real terror then the thing.

But now the happy hour appears,

That ſheaths the Sword , and cures our

   fears,

                    Now

Now is the Martial Trumpet dumb :

Sweet peace, sweet peace again is come !

So when the *Brutian* Sea doth rise,

By *Corus* driven to the Skys;

When from her Caverns *Scylla* raves,

Cust by the fury of the waves ,

And ships, though in their Haven, fear

Dreadfull *Caribdis* even there.

The sweating *Cyclops* when they spy

Waves o're their furnace *Ætna* fly,

Fear angry *Neptune* though their Sire,

VVill quench the never dying fire.

And poor *Laertes* trembling thinks

His little *Ithara* now sinks.

If the winds fall, the Sea appears

Smooth as the standing Pools, or Meers.

The trifling Boat now puts from shore :

Ships that like Islands seem'd, before

Were

Were not fo bold. Why name I thefe

Frail Barks? the floating *Cyclades*

Iflands like fhips, for motion thought,

Fear'd in the ftorm to be or'e wrought.

Yet now that Boat becalm'd, a fail

Puts up to catch the wanton Gale.

They the paft ftorms effects defcry,

And fee where drounded fifhes lye.

Fortunes ftill alter, none can laft:

Yet is the beft the fooneft paft.

The fwift viciffitudes of Fate

Can in a moment change our ftate.

He who doth Crowns difpofe, before

Whofe Throne all Nations do adore;

Intending, by a former Antecromifme, the *Roman* Emperor.

At whofe bare Nod the *Medes* difband:

Nor dare the *Indians* him withftand:

Nor

Nor *Daca* with their Cavalrie:

How full of anxious thoughts lives he?

What Changes do his fears, the while,

Presage from Fates inconstant smile?

Then swell no more; Great Souls of those

Where Heaven doth Soveraign Rule dif-
    pose:

Since that due Homage which we show

To you, ye to another owe.

The greatest Kings but Subjects be

To a Superior Majesty.

Some with that Sun have set, whose Ray

Shined at his Rise less bright then they.

Ah fading Joyes! In such who dare

Confide, or wanting them, despair?

Clotho with smiles doth Tears commix,

And lets no Chance of Fortune fix.

E 4   Heavens

Heavens greateſt Favorite can't ſay
I'le live and laugh another Day.
All our Affairs Fate troubles, and
Diſorders as : whirl·wind ſand.

ACT. IV.

Nuncius. Chorus.

Some Whirl-wind ſnatch me hence: by
  whoſe fierce ayd
I to th' obſcureſt Clowd may be convey'd,
VVhence I no more this curſed Houſe may
  ſee:
By *Tantalus* himſelf, abhor'd to be.
  Cho. Ha! what means this?———
    Nun. ———VVhat Country's this I
tread?
Argos, and *Sparta* is it, that hath bred
Such

Such bloudy Brothers? Live *Corinthians*
here

'Twixt thefe two Seas, or what I rather
fear,

Barbarous *Alani?* No *Hyrcanian* Breed

Of Tygers fure, nor *Scythians* thefe exceed.

    Cho. VVhat Salvage Crime blots our
unhappy Land

VVith fuch a Guilt? Give us to underftand.

    Nun. Can I my Senfes recollect, I will;

VVhen this cold Sweat fhall leave **my**
Limbs. For ftill

The horror follows me. —— Come ftorms
as ftrong

As my Defires, and bear me hence, along

VVhether the Sun flys from this fight away.

    Cho. You aggravate our fears by this
delay.

                Quickly

Quickly the Deed relate, and Author too.

Which of the Brothers is't? I ask not who.

  Nun.   In *Pelops* his chief Palace South-

ward lyes

A Part, that doth like some tall Mountain

rise

To pierce the Clouds, and o're the Town

doth stand,

Which should the same Rebell, it can Com-

mand :

There stands the Publick Hall, whose Roof

of Gold

Rich spotted Marble-pillars do uphold.

Besides this, where the Vulgar do repair,

Sev'ral as rich as spacious Rooms there are,

The privy Court i'th' uttermost Recess

Doth lye, by a Descent from the no less

Sacred

Sacred, then secret Grove divided there

Nor pleasant Trees nor profitable are,

But mournful Yew, Cypress, and Holm; ye
  higher

Then all the rest the tall Oak doth aspire,

And like a Prince o're looks the common

  Trees.

Our Kings do here consult their Auguries :

Here they seek Council when affairs appear

Doubtful or bad, Their Votive Guifts hang

  here :

Trumpets of War, and Trophys of the
  same,

With what by Land or Sea we overcame;

The vanquisht wheels, and treacherous Ax-
  el-Tree ,

And all our Nations Deeds, here fixed be.

                    Here's

Here's the *Tiara Phrygian Pelops* wore:

Here's what in War we took, or triumph
   bore.

Under this shade a Fountain stands, a Wave

So black and sad Dire *Styx* is said to have,

Dire *Styx* that binds the gods. The Fame's
   well-known

How here th' Infernal gods all Night do
   groan.

Clinking of Chains, howling of Ghosts,
   make here

A horrid noise; while what affrights the Ear

May there be seen : there haunt a Company

Of wandring souls which far more dreadfull be

Then common *Spectres*; sudden flames oft
   dart

Through all the Grove, and fix i'th' highest part.   Oft

Oft hath from thence three Barks at once been heard,

And oft the House with monstrous Visions scar'd,

Nor can the Day expel such fears; for there ever Night, and these at Noon appear.

Miraculous Resolves have here been found by them that seek, which with a frightfull sound

That fills the Place, arise from underground.

Then *Atreus* mad with Rage, was enter'd here,

Dragging his Nephews, deckt the Altars here.

Who with fit words can such black Deeds relate?)

Their Princely hands behind were pinnion'd streight,

Their

Their   Heads with purple fillets bound:
  there lyes
Ready both Incenfe for the Sacrifice,
And Wine, and Knife: ready prepar'd for it
Lies Salt and Meal. No Rite he doth omit,
Leaft not well done fhould be fuch wick-
  ednefs!

  Chorus. Who to their Execution dares
addrefs ?

  Nun. He is the Prieft himfelf : himfelf
doth Pray;
The Verficles of Death himfelf doth fay.
The Victims he in order placeth, and
Standing at th' Altar, takes the Sword in
  hand;
Himfelf attends, and doth omit no Rite:
This the Grove fees , and trembles at the
  fight.

                                    So

So doth the Ground, which shakes the
  House withall,

Whose Turrets doubtful on which side to
  fall

Nod every way; Also a Comet streams

From Heavens left side, which darts forth
  dismal beams.

The Wine as soon as cast into the flame,

VVas Transubstantiated, and blood be-
  came.

Oft his Crown fell: the Ivory Statues wept.

This all affrights; he still his temper kept;

And stands withall as if he'd terrifie

The threatning gods.———But all delays
  lay'd by,

He now ascends the Altar, with Oblique

Looks and Malevolent ; Some Tyger like

In *Ganges* Forreſt, whom fierce hunger
    fires,

Between two Steers that ſtands, and both
    deſires;

Yet unreſolv'd which firſt to ſeize; her eyes

That threaten De.th, to this, then that ap-
    plys;

With doubt as much as hunger next; And
    thus

On the Devoted looks Dire *Atreus.*

Revolving in his mind which ſhould be he

That firſt muſt fall; and which ſhould Se-
    cond be.

It matters not; yet takes he much delight

So high a Villany to Marſhal right.

    Chor. Which ſtrikes he then?

  Nun. ——————Parental Piety

Leaſt he ſhould want, firſt *Tantalus* muſt
dye.   T'his

T' his Grandfire dedicate.

  Cho.—— —— Oh fay, how took

The young Prince fuch a Death, and with
 what look?

   Nun. Carelefs of Life he ftands, and
doth refufe

In vain to fupplicate, or words to loofe.

But *Atreus* by the throat, him having tan'e

Sheaths in his Breaft the fword; which out
 again

Being redrawn, awhile the body thinks

How beft to fall, then on his Uncle finks.

Next *Plifthenes* he to the Altar brings,

And decollated, on his Brother flings:

Down proftrate falls the Trunk; and (with
 a found

Uncertain) the complaining head to th'
 ground.

       F   *Chor.*

Cher. What after this Twin-death doth he begin?

Spares he the child, or adds he sin to sin?

Nun. As a main'd Lyon equally repleat

With rage and hunger, sees a Heard of Neat

In the *Armenian* woods, pursues and takes

Many, whose blood his frowns more frightful makes:

Bulls do his hunger, not his Rage allay,

And after them he on the Calves doth prey,

With wearied Jaws: nor otherwise then so

Is *Atreus* cruel with his Rage; who though

His sword's distaind with double slaughter, yet

He seeks another murder to commit,

Careless on whom: In the childs breast he then

Strikes it, which out at s back appears agen.   He

He falls, his blood quenches the Altars
  fires;
Death enters at both wounds, and he at
  both expires.

  Chor. O barbarous act !

  Nun. ——— Doth this your horror breed ?
There's more behind, he stops not at this
  deed.

  Cho. Is there in Nature greater cruelty?

  Nun. Think you this all ? 'tis but the
firſt degree.

  Cho. What more? did he to beaſts their
bodys throw,
    And fire deny ?

  Nun. ——— Would he had only ſo !
Their Sepulture, and funeral Pile deny'd,
And caſt them out to birds of prey beſide,

Or with their flesh fed Wolves; what does
  appear

The greatest curse, had been a blessing here;

Their file to see them unenterr'd. —— O
  crime

Nor age will credit ! the insuing time

Will think this fabulous! their inward parts

He opens, their veins breathing still, and
  hearts

Still panting : thence the fates to recollect

He the warm veins, & Arterys doth dissect.

The Victims pleasing, now he time can
  spare

His brothers entertainment to prepare.

He cuts them out in joynts; close to their
  sides

The shoulders from the body he divides.

Their

Their tender flesh he from the bones doth
    pare :

Yet saves intire the heads, and hands which
    were

So lately sacred pledges. Th' Inwards
    they

Some spitted 'fore a slow fire drip away:

Some in the injured caldron boyl: while
    thefe

So horrid meats the very fire difpleafe,

Oft from the hearth it fell, & when return'd

Back to its place, it murmur'd as it burn'd.

The Livers screck upon the spit , nor well

Which moſt, the flesh or flames, groan'd,
    I tell.

The mournful fire in clowds of smoak con-
    fumes :

And even thofe heavy clowds and ominous
    fumes   F 3   Directly

Directly not afcend, as wont, but fly

About the houfhold gods, & there they lye.

O patient *Phæbus* ! though day backward
    flys,

And though thy luftre at the Zenith dyes,

Thou fet'ft too late. —— His Sons the Fa-
    ther eats,

And his own Limbs are his Inhumane
    treats :

While with rich Unguents his hair fhines,
    and he

Sits full of mighty Wine, unwillingly

Difcends the barbarous dyet. Only this

Of good, *Thyeftes* 'mongft thy Evills is,

You know 'em not : yet even this will fade.

Though *Titan* turns his Chariot, which is
    made

                          To

To meafure back the way it came ; though
   Night

With fhades unufual hides this deed from
   fight ,

Which from the Eaft doth rife, and out
   of time;

Yet will at laft be feen each horrid crime,

Chorus.

Father of gods and men, at whofe

Uprife Night doth her beauty loofe,

Whether, O whether doft thou ftray,

And at thy Noon benight the day ?

What frights thee, Sun? not yet appears

Vefper the harbinger of ftars :

Nor *Hefper* fhining in the weft

Bids thy diurnal Chariot reft :

Nor

Nor the third Trumpets found yet made

A welcome to th' approaching shade.

Amazed the Plowman stands to see

Day end, untired his Team and he.

What stops thy Race? what is't do's make

Thy *Steeds* their beaten Road forsake?

Do now from hel the Gyants rise

Again to fight the Deitys?

His old Attempts doth *Tytius* strive,

With his first fury, to revive?

Hath now *Typhæus* freed his breft,

Long with the Mountains weight opprest?

Or do the gods *Phlegræan* foes

Offa on *Pelion* now impose? ——

All the known course of time is done!

No more will set or rise the Sun.

Days Mother with Nocturnal dew's

Still wet, while now she *Phæbus* views

As

As to her East he back retires,
Whence he so lately went, admires.
How ignorant is she to lave
His steeds in the refreshing wave!
He stands surpriz'd too, since to this
New Inne himself a stranger is.
The morning Sun now sets, whose light
Yeilds to a darknels, yet no night;
On his Recels no stars appear:
Nor fire shines in our Hemisphere.
No Moon adorns these shades. Whate're
This is, Night would it only were.
Each heart with suddain fear possest
Doth tremble, tremble in each breast,
Least all should ruin'd be; least men
And even the gods themselves, agen
To their old *Chaos* fall: left fire
And sea, Earth and Heavens gay attire

Of

Of sparkling stars, should now return

To their first nothing. ——No more burn

Shall thy bright flames, nor *Phœbus,* thou

Be longer chief of Plannets, now,

Summer and winter, nor shall we

Distinguish by the Course of thee.

No more shall the pale Queen of shades

Expel that fear which Night invades,

While she in a less Circle runs,

And ends her Race before the Suns.

Into but one deform'd lump shall

The Elements and Plannets fall.

Heavens bless the *Zodiac,* whose bright way

Shines with the Lights of night and day,

Whose Circle parts the *Zones,* and we

Measure the Year by its Degree,

Shall fall from Heaven, and with it then

These stars set, ne'r to rise agen :

First

Firſt ſhall the Ram, who us'd to bring

Soft weſtern Gales with the kind ſpring,

Plunge in thoſe waves o're which he bore

The trembling *Helle* heretoſore.

Next ſhall the *Bull* deſcend, between

Whoſe bright horns are the *Hyads* ſeen;

And draw the Twins and *Crab* along

With him from the Cæleſtial throng.

The *Lyon* then ſhall down again

Return, and no more ſcorch the Grain.

Down from her heaven the *Virgin* ſhall

Along with her the ballance fall:

With them ſhall the fierce *Scorpion* go,

And he arm'd with th' *Æmonian* bow:

Old *Chiron*, in his fall who will

His Quiver break, and arrows ſpill.

The winter-leading *Goat* muſt be

The next, and falling break ſhall he

Thy

Thy water-pot, who er'e thou art :

With thee the *Fishes* shall depart

Last of the Twelve.   The Bears that ner'e

Set in the waves, shall now drownd there.

The *Snake* that those two Bears divides,

And like a crooked River glides,

Shall as all other Rivers, roule

Into the sea. While from the Pole

Cold *Cynosure* the lesser Bear

Plac'd by the greater *Dragon* there,

With whom *Bootes,* flow-pac'd swain

Shall fall, and drive from Heaven his Wain.

Selected from Mankind, do we

This fatal period live to see ?

Must the world fall on us ? O Fate

Wretched and most unfortunate!

Whether we loose without offence

The *Sun,* or guilty, drive him hence :

Yet

Yet ceaſe to mourn: there is no need.

He's covetous of Life indeed

Who longer to ſurvive deſires,

VVhen the whole Univerſe expires.

ACT. V.

Atreus.

Now equal to the ſtars I walk, now I

Look down, methinks, on others from the

   sky.

My Fathers Throne, and Ram, I've now

   regain'd,

I've done with Heaven: and my laſt wiſh

   attain'd.

Tis very well; exceeding well; and this

Revenge even for me ſufficient is.——

                     But

But why sufficient? I'le proceed, and fill

VVith his own blood *Thyeſtes* fuller ſtill.

Left I ſhould ſee , and bluſh at this black

deed

The day retires : VVhile Heaven invites,

proceed.

VVould the fled god's might be forc'd

back by me,

That they this banqnet of Revenge might

ſee !

Yet ſhall the Father: and let that ſuffi ce.

This darkneſs that now hides his miſeries

I will diſſolve, though day refuſe.   Gueſt

mine,   (lyne

Thou haſt too long careleſs and chearful

You've eat and drunk enough. *Thyeſtes*

needs

Be ſober rightly to reſent ſuch deeds:

                        Wine

VVine drounds his fence. ———— So there
within, who waits :

Display the Feaft, open the Temple gates.

I long to fee , when his Sons heads he
views,

How he will look, or what expreffions ufe

To fpeak his grief; or how (his fpirit's loft

At this) hee'l ftand as if congeal'd with
froft.

This is my deed : To fee him wretched, no
Delight take I, but in his making fo.

The Scene opens, and

Thyeftes is Difcovered.

Behold the Room with many Lights array'd:

On Gold and Purple he fupinely lay'd;

On

On his left hand , his head opprest with
   Wine   (shine

He leans, and belches.   Now methinks I

Chief of the Gods, and King of Kings ! In
   this

I have o'pass my wish. —— See, see, he is

Already full; from a large Goblet he

Drinks unmixt VVine : Drink on; I've
   still for thee

One Cup, the blood of the late sacrifice:

The colour of Red wine shall this disguize.

And let this Cup conclude this Feast. He
   mine

Did thirst , who now shall drink commixt
   with VVine

His Childrens blood. —— Hark; he to sing
   prepares,

Unable to contain his Joy, light Ayrs.

                           Thyestes

Thyestes.

Thou that so dull'd with sufferings art,

Cast off thy busy Cares, my heart.

Hence grief, hence fear, and thou er'e while

My old Companion in Exile

Sad Poverty ; hence thou that late

Didst vex my soul, of my low state

A conscious shame ; of that no more

I le think, but what I was before.   ·

'Tis brave when fall'n from high Command,

Firm and unmoved below to stand.

Opprest with mighty Ills, 'tis rare

And brave, with neck unbow'd to bear,

Of a lost Kingdom the sad weight ;

Nor conquer'd, nor degenerate,

G

But

But to ſtand upright under thoſe

Unwelcome preſſures Fates impoſe.

Theſe clouds that now thy ſoul or'e caſt,

And all the marks of miſery paſt

Caſt off, and to thy face once more

The ſmiles of ſoft content reſtore :

From thy grieved memory let paſs

The old *Thyeſtes*. But alas !

·Tis proper to th' unfortunate

Never to truſt the ſmiles of fate.

Though happineſs return again,

Joy is to them a kind of pain. ——

What grief is this obſtructs my mirth

From no known cauſe that takes its birth ?

This day of Feſtival to keep

What hinders me, and bids me weep ?

With odorous flowr's my head t' array

What is't doth thus, doth thus gainſay?

The

The Roses from my brows descend,

And my p erfumed hair stands on end

With suddain horrour; while apace

Sad streams or'e flow a chearful face.

My mirth with groans is often checkt ;

And my late tears I still affect:

So fond the wretched ever be

To doat on their old misery.

Mournful complaints fain would I vent,

And tear this purple ornament

Oft-times our souls prophetick be,

And droop with sorrows they fore-see.

So when the Sea to swell doth use,

And no wind breaths, a storm insues. —

Mad man ! thy mind why thus dost thou

Disturb, and discompose thy brow?

Thy Brother trust: now what er'e fate

Befalls, fears causeless, or too late.

Thus

Thus timerous I would not be

But a strange terror troubles me

Within, which through my eyes doth pour

A causeless, and surprizing showr'.

Sorrows effect is this or fears?

Or hath great Joy its proper tears?

          Atreus (*going to him*)

Brother, with joynt consent let's celebrate

This day; that will confirm my Regal state

And 'twixt us two settle a lasting peace.

     Thy. I'me cloyd with wine and feasting;

    'twould increase

My pleasure, and no small addition be

To my full Joy, could I my Children see.

          Atreus (*ambiguously.*)

Be confident they'r in your armes, for here

They are, and shall be; do not fear.

                 Nothing

Nothing of thine ſhal be withheld: You ſhall

Their deſired preſence now enjoy, I all ʃ

Of thee with thy ſo loved Iſſue will,

Doubt not, moſt fully ſatisfie and fill.

At preſent with my Sonʃ they celebrate

This day of Joy: but I will call 'em ſtraight

Firſt taſt our Familieʃ cup fi l'd with choice

   wine.

     Thy. Brother, I kindly take this guiſt

'cauſe thine.

Firſt offer to our Fathers deities;

And then wee'l drink —— How's this ? my

   hand denies

Her office : ſtill the wines weight heavier

   grows,

And loads my arm; while from my Lips it

   flows :

        G 3   About

About my mouth it rouls, nor down will
   go,

See the ground shakes; the Table too doth
   so.

The fire it self scarce shines: on the Suns
   flight,

The Sky stands Neutral betwixt day and
   night.——

How's this? Heavens connex sinks still lower and lower:

To darkness joyns a darkness that is more
Condenst, and night it self to this is day.
Each star is fled. What e're this means, I pray
That from my Brother, and my Sons it be
Averted, and the Omen threaten me.
Restore me now my Sons.

   Atr. —— I will restore,
And they from thee shall ne're be parted
   more.   *Thy*

Thy. What tumult shakes me thus within? My breast

Is with a sad impatient weight opprest:

Sad groans I with a voice not mine respire.

Appear my Sons, your most unhappy sire

Bids you appear : your sight alone will cure

This grief. —— Whence answer they ?

    Atr. ——— Make ready your

                      (Shews the Heads)

Embraces: they are come, —Now Sir, do ye know

    Your Sons ? ———

    Atr. I know my Brother.—— Canst thou undergo,

Dull earth, such wickedness, & bear it thus?

And not to *Styx* sink both thy self and us?

Wilt thou not open that these Kingdoms may

And King, through thee to *Chaos* find a way?
           G 4   Wilt

Wilt thou not all the ſtructures of this Land

Levell with their foundations? We to ſtand

Both well deſerve in hell with *Tantalus,*

And other the Progenitors of us,

If any there. Open now, open wide

Thy diſlocated Joynts on every ſide,

Down let us ſink through ſome vaſt cleft
  of thee

To *Acheron,* and there for ever be.

While or'e our heads th' Infernal ſhapes
  appear,

Flow hither *Phlegethon,* and ſetling here,

Us wretches in thy flaming waters drownd.

Lyeſt thou unmoved ſtill, dull ſenceleſs
  ground ?

  Atr. Here, take thy Sons, ſo much deſired by thee :

Enjoy them now, there's no delay in me :

Each

Each of these three alike embrace and kiss.

Thy. Is this thy League? thy amity? is
this   (have

A Brothers faith? Thus dost thou love? To
Safe or alive, my Sons, I do not crave :
This I thy brother beg, which no ways your
Revenge impleads, allow them sepulture.
I ask but what I le burn : 'tis nothing I
Beg to enjoy, but part with by and by.

    Atr. All of thy Sons I'le give, that I
did save :
What not remains, that you already have.

    Thy. Lye they a Feast for Birds of
Prey? or are   (fare?
They for wild beasts reserv'd inhumane

    Atr. Thou of thy Sons hast made that
impious feast.

    Thy. 'Twas this that sham'd the gods'
his to the East   Forc'd

Forc'd back the Sun!wretch that I am what

    crys,   (suffice?

What sad complaints, what words will me

Their heads and hands chopt off too plain

    I see,   (be.

And from their Legs how their feet sever'd

'Twas the presage of this unheard of meat,

Though pinch'd with hunger,would not let

    me eat.

My bowels roul about,and seek with pain

A passage for the horrid food, in vain.

Lend me thy sword dyed in my blood,and I

Will to my Sons with it give liberty.

Is this deny'd?yet shall with frequent blows

This breast resound ; ah, no ! forbear from

    those

Unhappy man,and spare the dead within—

Hath ever such a curst deed acted been

                          By

By barbarous *Heniochan* that's bred

On *Caucasus* ? or the *Cecropian* dred

Procrustes? oh! my Sons do me oppress,

And I my Sons,---No mean in wickedness

   Atr. A mean should be observ'd when

   first we act

A wrong, but not when we revenge a fact.

This is but small for me. I should have shed

Goar in thy mouth as from the wound it

   bled: (thou

That of thy living Sons , the warm blood

Mightst drink: I've trifled with my anger

   now.

In hast I gave the wounds, Of them I made

A sacrifice, I the vow'd slaughter payd

To my wrong'd houshold gods; and jointing

   all

Their livelels bodies into goblets smal,

                      I

I rent each Limb: and fome of them I caft
Into the boiling Cauldron, fome I plac't
By a flow fire to roft. They not yet dead
I cut their Nerves, and members quar-
tered:
I heard the Inwards groan upon the fpit:
I my felf made the fire and lookt to it.
All this their Father better might have
done !
My Rage is fpent in vain. 'Tis true each
Son
Of his, his curfed mouth did tear and eat,
But both the Eater ignorant, and meat.

   Thy. Ye Seas with wandring fhores in-
compaffed,
Hear this! Here this you gods, where-
ever fled !

Hear this hell! Earth hear this! and thou
  Night made

More black and horrid by a hellish shade,

Attend to what I'le say, and what is said:

Darkness I'me left to thee, and only thou

Sad as my self, canst view my sorrows now.

No suppliant vows for my concern I'le
  make.

Ah! what is that? Nature 'tis for thy sake.

Great King of Gods, who the Worlds
  Soveraign art,   (part

Bury the Earth in Clouds from every

Bid the winds fight, and thou thy Thun-
  : [der dart.

Use not that hand which lesser bolts do
  throw

To batter guiltless buildings here below :

                              But

But with that hand that levell'd Mountains
    rear'd

Three stories high, & Gyants that appear'd

Like other Mountains upon them: on us

Discharge thy Lightning and thy thunder
    (thus.

Make good the perish't day. Let thy fires
    fly:

The light that's lost with lightning now
    ' supply.

Doubt not of us whose cause doth call,
    they be

Both bad: if not, yet mine is; aime at me,

Transfix this breast with thy Artillery.

To their last fire would I my Sons bestow;

My self into those Funeral flames must go.

If nothing moves the Gods, if sinners they

Neglect to punish : Night, for ever stay

                And

And hide our Crime; *Titan* I'le nere com-
plain

So thy bright flames no more return again.

   Atr. Now I applaud my hands; the
Palm I've won.

I' had loft my glory thus had I not done.

Now my bed chaft I think , and Children
mine.

    Thy. Why fhould the Infants dye;

Atr. For being thine.

    Vhy. With his own Sons doft thou
the Father feaft ?

    Atr· Ay, the undoubted Sons, which
pleafes beft.

    Thy. Witnefs ye Gods.————

   Atr.——The Nuptial Powers well may.

   Thy. With a worfe Deed who would a
Crime repay ?

Atr.

Atr. I know what grieves you. To prevented be

Your next; not what thou haft devour'd moves thee,

But not t' have dreft the fame. Thou didft defign,

Ignorant, fuch Viands fhould be mine:

Their Mother helping, thou did'ft mean to feife

My Sons, and butcher them as I did thefe:

You'd don't, but that you fancy'd them your own.

Thy. Be prefent ye juft Gods: to them alone

I give thee up for Punifhment. ——

Atr. ——— ——— ——— For it

I to thy Childrens Manes thee commit.

FINIS.

MOCK-THYESTES.

ACT. I.

TANTALUS. MEGÆRA.

Tant. What Witch of *Endor* does thus
    fret me.

And when I'de ftay in hell won't let me'?

Cannot a man be damn'd in quiet,

But *Haggs* muft thus commit a Riot?

You'l whip me out of Hell-doors we' ye?

And firk me up, with a *Pox* te' ye?

I muft to earth: but pray let's know

What I muft do there er'e I go.

I cannot teach 'em damning there,

Nor more debauch 'em then they are,

To Wench, drink, rook, or be uncivil,

They scorn to learn of a poor Devill.

'Tis ten to one the *Sons of Whores*

Will either kick me out of doors ,

Or think me a tame harmless *Cully*,

And then I'me gone to *Nicker-Bully*.

But should I take a Wenches shape,

'Tis six to four I get a *Clap*.

And then how shamefully 'twill urge one,

That comes from *Hell* to use a *Surgeon?*

All that I say I can make good

In mine own proper flesh and blood.

Two *Imps* I have as very *Rakells*

As er'e did cling in *Newgate* shackles:

Men call one *Atreus*, and the other

Thyestes , *Atreus*'s own *Brother*.

Rake *Hell*, and skim the *Devill*, if er'e

You match 'em, I'le be hang'd; that's fair.

Meg.

Meg. Allons; and ſtand not thus hum

drum:

Or Faith I'le run this Pin i' your bum.

De'e think I'le ſuffer you, conclude

Whether the thing be bad or good ?

Yet if you wonder at your Miſſion,

And why 'tis with ſuch expedition ;

To give your *Nephews* a kind Viſit,

If you would know the true cauſe, is it.

Oh then, and do juſt as I tell ye':

Firſt put two live Eels in their belly,

Which may ſo operate, and frisk it,

As if old *Nick* were in their *Brisket.*

Where Nature's dull, we thus muſt force

her:

(For *Devils* may learn of a *Horſe-Courſer*)

Then make 'em hector, huff, and ſwear,

Curſe, damn, and ſink, ſpit, fire, and ſtare;

Snatch

Snatch Spits and tilt at one another,

And *Brother* bite off Nose of *Brother.*

  Tan. I, say you so? but if you get me

To do't, I le give you leave to eat me.

Perhaps on earth what you have moved,

Is often done, and well approved;
And to debauch ones own *Relation*

Counted a *Genteil Recreation.*

But soft, you ne're sh ll get me to it;

An honest *Devil* will not do it.

Do you my *Grandchildren* suppose

Bull-Doggs to run full at the Nose?

Or think you them *Cocks*, grown so sullen

To spit themselves instead of *Pullen?*

In *fine*, I tell you once again,

Tempt me no more; for 'tis in vain.'

  Meg. Well, since I can't this way prevail,

I le try now to perswade your *Tail,*

                  Your

Your *Toby* I'le fo feaze with this
Rod that has lain three weeks in pifs,
That you fhall begg the thing to do,
Before we part, and thank me too.
Come, come, untrufs; or muft I force ye,
And call *Tyfiphone* to horfe ye?

  Tant. Oh lay that frightfull Engine by.

         (*Kneels.*

Dred Queen, for if it fhakes I dye.
And I will your Commands obey,
Like your moft humble —— as they fay.
But fpare my buttocks, let me begg ye;
For they are tender, deareft *Megge.*

  Meg. Enough, I pardon: do not doubt it,
But let's fhake hands, and fo about it.

  Tan. Like a dire Vapour, which fome call
A *Blaft Hypocondriacal:*

      H 3   Or

Or like the steem of Candle snuff
I come, but peacably enough;
Then fear not *Mortals*, I will do
No harm, but stink, and so adiew.

Madam, when you confer the Grace
Next, your Command on me to place,
Henceforth I'le do it without grudging:
And like a plain well-meaning *Gudgin*.
What er'e you offer me I'le swallow.
Go on sweet *Lady*, for I follow.

Exeunt.

Chorus.

If any of the Starry *Powers*
Value one pin, or us, or ours:
If *Jupiter* or *Mars* ere saw
A *Miss* among us worth a straw,

If

If we have ought that's worth their care

Twixt wind and water, or elfe where

I wish with all my heart and Soul

That they our *Quarrels* would controul.

For this fame *Atreus* and *Thyeſtes*

Are both ſtark naught who er'e the beſt is.

Cat after kind exact: 'Tis plain

That neither of 'em croſs the ſtrain.

Pelops their Father was, and he

Kill'd his own Wives *Dad a dadde.*

He loved the Sport ſo well that rather

Then want a Wench he'd kill a Father.

Nay more, the moſt ungrateful Woer

Hang'd the poor *Pimp* that helpt him to
  her.

Now if the *Heraulds* books don't fail us,

Pelops was Son of one *Tantalus;*

He was, as is reported common,

Of *London Town* a Serjeants Yeoman ;

Who to arreſt a Cook, once came

In place *Ram Ally* call'd by name :

Some *Clerks* and *Bullies* of the Cloiſters

Were there by chance then opening 'Oy-

ſters :

Theſe ſeeing their *Cook* in woſul danger,

On whom they lay at Rack and manger:

Or as ſome ſay, 'twas chiefly 'cauſe

They ſaw a Rupture in the Laws,

And ſacred Franchiſe of the Ally;

They never ſtand ye ſhally ſhally,

But take poor *Tant* and hurl him in

To Temple *Bog-houſe* up to th' Chin.

But here the Miſchief ends not yet

(To ſee a Cooks malicious wit!)

When

When *Tant* had stood there half a day,

He thought him hungry, as we say,

His Knife unto the Spit he puts ye,

And pen'worth six of Roast Beef cuts ye;

In order then to what his heart meant,

He runs me strait to *Tants* appartment.

There holding it down in the Hole,

He cry's you cursed Dog *Catchpole*,

Look what is here, do's your Maw crave it?

'Yes, when y' are hang'd then you shall
    have it.

This said, in an heroick strain,

His hand he snatches up again.

Then brings the flagon full of Ale,

Or as some *Authors* have it, *Stale.*

For Flagons oft have used been

Both to fill out, and empty in.

Or

Or as the plain expreffion is,

Either to drink in, or to pifs,

Now (as all Cooks do ofte n try)

Hot ftinks do make men develifh dry,

The cunning Spit-man therefore, thus

Brings a full Pot to *Tantulus* :

Which wheh the poor Fool reaches at,

He empties it upon his Pate,

And this is briefly the firft rifing

Of that which we call *Tantalizing.*

A C T. II.

Enter Atreus, *and a Servant.*

A *Treus.* 'Tis true, my *Brother* did feduce
My *Sponfe,* but that's not all th'abufe.
For

For *Jack* as I was saying, if he
Had done this out of *Amity*
And pure good will unto my Wife,
It had ner'e griev'd me, but, us'd life!
To Cuckold me out of meer scorn,
By flesh and blood cannot be born.

  Sei. That's very true. But still I say Sir,
How if it were in a fair way Sir?

  Atr. Lord *Jack*, thou art just such ano-
    ther: ———

When the thing's cleer to make a puther?
For look ye, *Fenny*, had she been
As beauteous as is any Queen,
Then it might well have been as you say;
But she's as ugly as *Medusa*.
'Twas therefore done you plainly see,
In spight, and disrespect to me.

                    And

And now, dear Rogue, let think upon't:

For I·le not put up the affront.

    Ser.Muſt my Dame too be guilty made?

For ſhe was in the *Mu∫querade*——

Couchant, and did, as I may ſay,

Act her own part in the foul *Play*.

Muſt ſhe then ſhare in the Purgation,

As well as in the Recreation?

    Atr. No *Jack*, my Wife's my Wife, and

  ſhe

Muſt be indulg'd as part of me.

Peſides all Women, if you mind,

Have weaker Veſſels then Mankind,

More frail, and therefore not a little

Apt to be crackt, and very brittle.

On this account your pritty Laſſes

Have been compar'd to *Venice Glaſſes*.

                And

And should we Husbands sume and fret

For every Rap our Spouses get;

'Twould be most redicule, and he

That does it, not at all jentee.

Then lastly know, we both dispence

With one another, in this sence.

And both have Conscience-Liberty

By Joint-consent of her and me,

To solace in a Modish manner,

And she not Curse me, nor I ban her.

But though my Wife goes Scotfree here,

I'le make it cost my *Brother* dear.

Now honest *Jack*, I pray you kindly,

Advise how I may do it finely.

   Ser. Ah, Master, I'me but simply learned

To be in things of Weight concerned.

But since ye 'are pleas'd to have my answer,

To this I'le do the best I can Sirs.

VVhat

What if we too, and a third Man
Should catch him Napping when we can;
And then e'ne geld him for a warning?
This sure will spoil his Trade of Horning.

Atr. But should I mayhem him in this
  sort,
And then be bring his *Action* for 't.
What Damage Juries may impose
For such a Carving, Heaven knows.

Ser. Then let him; since th' offence was
  done
In blankets, be well tost in one.
And so the business shall be ended
In the same manner he offended.

Atr. Well, should I like your way; but
  this
Too violent and open is.

I would some private trick invent
To give him a sound punishment,
And yet he ner'e the wiser for it.
As for the Triumph, I abhor it.

   Ser. Why then, Sir thus: you need but
    stay
Till he too Marry's, and you may
By amorous Retaliation,
Debauch his Wife in the same fashion.
Thus you shall have Sir, (when you doe't)
Revenge, and a fresh Girl to boot.

   Atr. I like this better then all yet:
But, *Jonney*, here's the Devill of it,
Delay in these things is so hellish,
It dulls the Sport, and palls the Relish.
Revenge and Love should both advance
Sa, Sa, in the brisk aire of *France*,———

I feel a rumbling in my belly
To do a thing which I won't tell ye.
Sure 'tis some Spirit that thus puts
Me on, and agitates my Guts.
Well I will on, and never fear it,
Since 'tis a motion of the Spirit.
And Spirits less Fanatique are
In belly then in brain, by far.
Jack, run, and send some idle Boy
To you know who with this Envoy:
That howsoer'e my Carriage past
May give him cause of some distast,
I humbly begg now to be Friends,
And for those honest Golden Ends
Beseech him that he would not fail
To come and tast of my Wives *Ale*,
And when he comes it shall go hard
But something else shall be prepar'd.

You.

You underſtand me *Jack? Ser.* Yes Maſter:

Atr. I prithee run a little faſter ——

Yet ſtay. A looſe *Boy* may betray us;

I'le ſend my own Sons *Menelaus;*

And *Agamemnon* with a Letter:

And that will do a great deal better.

Exeunt.

Chorus.

Methinks theſe are but odd *Caprices*

To make two Brothers fall a peeces,

And quarrel for ſo poor a thing

As is a little Cuckolding.

And what de'e think Sirs, all this while;

Is that which makes ſo great a Coil?

But a meer empty Name! For the thing

Was never ſeen by any breathing,

I   Nor

Nor felt, nor heard; and why then shou'd
This word dare to be understood?

'Tis but an *Embryo* miscarriage:
It is the Maiden-head of Marriage;
And Maiden-heads for ought I can see,
Only consist in a strong Fancy.

Then Cuckoldy and Pusillage
Are but two shaddows of the Age.

Twixt which the difference is not great:
A single and a double Cheat.

And yet for this men take the pains
To beat out one anothers brains.
Nor do they spare the other Sex,
But often break their Spouses necks.
Then happy she, whose Husband's wary,
And keeps her caged like Bird-Canary,
Giving her once a day, with care,
Linseed and water, fresh and fair.

Un-

Unknown to Town-wits, and unknowing

Coaches, she spends her time in sewing.

Or else in spinning, or in knitting:

And has her belly full of sitting.

But she that is for Beauty famous,

And knows a man, abroad, from a Mouse.

Whose fine *French* carriage never wants

Variety of fresh Gallants.

Much Love without doors while she gets,

Causing within more jealous heats,

May dye of Husbands bangs perhaps:

If not, yet of her Servants Claps.

ACT. III.

Enter *Thyestes*, with a Bagg
in his Hand.

Tis good before I further go,
        To think if it were best or no.

Or (as I read once in a Book)

Before I take my leap to look.
The scruples then which in my brain lye
I'le open legally, and plainly.
The Case is thus. *A.* lies with *B.*

I. S.'s Wife: *I: S.* sends *C*

To *A* with formal Invitation

To come and tast of a Collation.

A. doubts *I. S.* is double hearted,

Or (if you'l have it word-of-arted)

A

A meer Trapanner, and demurring,

Is not o're hasty to be stirring.

The Points are two. First whether *A*,

Should go: or, Secondly, shou'd stay,

The Case being thus stated, hark ye

How all the Parts about me argue,

In the first place, my head cries tarry;

For should he break me you'd be sorry;

'Tis more then likely he forgets not

How you us'd his head:though he frets not,

Nor shews resentment by much huffing

Yet he may pay all off with cuffing.

My back and sides have the same fears

For bangs: so have for lugs my ears.

Now on the other side, my belly

Saies go,or else the Devil quel ye;

There will be Viands choice and dainty;

And of good Bub no doubt great plenty.

My

My Guts will fwim in lufhious Seas
Of Ale as ftrong as *Hercules.*

My Eyes cry, on; and leave your fears:
Or elfe wee'l drow'nd our felves in Tears:
But if you go, we hope once more
To fee his Wife, that honeft Whore.
And there's another part of mine
That's mad with the felf-fame defign.
My members being thus divided,
Now hang me if I can decide it. ——
But look: while here I ftand and ponder,
Some body comes to meet me yonder.
'Tis he himfelf with a clean Band on.
This is an honour, and a Grand one !

   Enter Atrcus.

 Atr. My dear *Thyeftes!* *Thy.* Deareft
Dear !   *(Embrace.*
Atr. How glad am I to fee you here:
        Thy.

Thy. And how does all at home Boy?
Cranky?

Atr. All reasonably well, I thank ye——

Thy. But how, but how, does your good
Wife?

Atr. Oh, lusty (as they say) for life:
As brisk, as jolly, and as ayrie
As a young Kitlin, or a Fary.

Thy. And how does all your Children,
lastly:
And honest *Towser* the old Masty?

Atr. All at your Service, my dear Sweeting.

Thy. Lord, how yo' are alter'd since last
meeting
Methinks you're grown more tall & bony.
But for those *Breeches*, I'de not known ye.

Atr. Brother, once more I'me glad to see ye:
And if ye' ad brought your Puss-Cats wi.
ye   I 4   My

My happineſs had been compleat.

　　Thy. Sweet Sir, if that will do the Feat;
They're in this bagg, and at your ſervice.

　　Atr. More welcome then Sun-ſhine in

　Harveſt;

Then nine a clock to Prentice boys
In winter nights; or Marriage-Joyes
To crooked Virgins, is each Puſs
To, Sir, your Servant *Atreus*.
But wherefore are they thus convey'd,
Like Pig in Pocket——Maſquerade?

　Thy. To let 'em beat upon the hoof
Thus far, had merited reproof.
For ſurely *Brother*, it is fitting
They ride when they go a Viſiting,
Therefore to ſave their feet a labour,
I ſtole this Cock-bagg of a Neighbour:

　　　　　　　　　　　　And

And it as well serves their turn, for ought
I see, as a guilt Coach or Chariot.

Atr. 'Tis very true —— But see, we'are
come
To the Frontier that is, ee'n at home.
Repose a while, pray, in the inner
Parler, and I'le go hasten Dinner.

Exeunt.

Chorus.

How suddainly these Brothers twain
Fell out? how soon they'r Friends again?
Could any man alive imagine
Peace after such a huff and raging?
Well: though I say't that should not say't,
True Love cannot be long in hate.

So have I seen (as Poets say)

Domestick Dudgeon in a Fray.

When Coblers Wife 'gainst Cobler, for

Prerogative, denounces War.

Cob calls *Tib* Bitch, aud takes his stirrup

With which he vows he will firk her up.

But *Tib* as valerous as a Lass

As er'e *Penthesilea* was,

Scorns to turn Tail on any man,

But bids him do the worst he can:

Then snatches up a basting Ladle.

With which she vows to break his Nodle.

And to defend her self from him,

Takes for a buckler her Wheel Rim.

Thus arm'd, they both begin the fight

With all the Conduct requisite.

Fury had but a while run loose,

When *Cob* was glad to begg a Truce:

And

And *Tib*, who was no Jew nor Heathen,
Granted a time we call a breathing.
Now *Cob* takes up his Awle and Pinfer,
As the beſt Weapon to convince her.
Tib changes hers too, and thinks fit
To play it out at ſingle Spit.
So ſkilfully ſhe Fenc'd and Parry'd,
That the poor Cuckold ſhe ſoon weari'd.
At length when Female Rage wat ſpent,
Tib to a Treaty does conſent.
Then over half a dozen of ſtale——
Beer, or perhaps Beer and Ale,
Which *Cob* had ſacrific'd to Peace,
All's well again ; and Diſcords ceaſe.
Thus 'twixt the Brothers it has been;
Firſt they fall out, and then fall in.
O what a *Jilt* is *Gammer Fortune* ?
No Weather-cock is more uncertain.

A

A Spinster of so rough a hand,

That when her work seems at a stand,

She gives her Wheel a whisk o'th' suddain,

And stirs all round like Hasty Pudden.

ACT. IV.

Nuncius. Chorus.

CHo, Pray Master *Nuncius*, what does

  vex ye?

If one may be so bold to ax' ye.

 Nun. Oh! heavy News as happen'd ere

yet !

So heavy I can scarcely bear it.

 Cho. Ah well away, this does so quell me

I could e'en cry, before you tell me.

But

But let us hear it, with your favour,

How bad fo er'e the Tale does favour.

   Nun. For Loves fake tarry but a little,

And you fhall know it ev'ry tittle.

I'me one that need but little dunning:

Only I'me out of breath with running.

Aye me. Alas, alas , Highoe.——

Sirs, in the firft place you muft know,

There were three dainty Tabby Cats

Thyeftes loved as well as *Brats.*

Nay fure no *Chuck* nor *Child* could be

So dear to him as were thefe three,

I, and they were fuch pretty Creatures,

No *Mifs* could match dear *Pufs* for Fea-

  tures.

Sweetly they'd pur, and briskly they

  Would lye upon their backs, and play.

But if by chance they caught a Moufe

Lord! how they'd dance about the houfe?

And having found the little Ceeature,

They allwaies courfe her er'e they eat her.

While Noble fport *Thyeftes* found

'Twixt *Mufs* the Hare, & *Pufs* Grayhound.

Now when our Neighbour Gaffer *Atreus*

Seem'd to his Brother very gracious:

Late fending to *Thyeftes* Greeting,

He bid him to a merry Meeting;

To which his welcome fhould be fuch,

That even his Dog fhould have as much:

His love to him was fo fincere,

That any thing of his was dear.

This was his Meffage; and ith' end on't——

Pray bring along the *Cur* appendant.

At this *Thyeftes* heart was truly,

Soft as *May-Butter* is in *July*:

And

And melted down into his breeches,

To hear his *Brothers* kind beseeches.

But being well Educated, he

Did in this manner Repartee.

He tells him first that he will come;

But fears to be too troublesome.

Next, with due thanks, he does confess

He keeps no Dog, nor great nor less.

A Leash of Cats, indeed, he ner'e wants,

And they are his most humble Servants.

The Messenger a man of Honour,

Reply'd in this obliging manner.

He loves a Puss as well as any :

Bring all your Cats though ner'e so many.

And when you are at Dinner set,

They shall be into th' Dayry let;

Where they new Milk & Cream shall lap:

I, and some Firmity perhap.

Chor.

Chor. This was all done *en Chevalier*.

    Nun. True, but the sad Tale ends not

here.

Thyestes comes, as he was pray'd,

With his Retinue abovesaid.

Atreus in very civil fashion

Gives him a kind Accomodation,

Pray take a seat, quoth he, I'le wait

Upon you, dearest *Brother*, strait.

VVhen out, the door he opening wide,

Beckons the Kittins a to side.

Suspecting nought, they follow; whom

He leads into a Drawing Room,

Which was a neat convenient place

Contriv'd just under the stair-case.

VVhen seeing his advantage pat,

He snickles up the Eldest Cat.

                        While

While the reft wonder what the man ment,

Efteeming this coarfe Entertainment,

He hits me one full on the Sconce

With a *Battoon* made for the nonce.

So well the blow he re-inforc'd

That *Pufs* muft needs give up the Ghoft;

Had her Nine Lives been twenty one

Her Leafe was now not worth a bone.

In *fine*, he kill'd the other laftly,

Though the poor Creature look't moft
    Gaftly.

Cho. O *Ruthfull Act!* —— *Nun.* 'Twas
fad indeed:

But fadder that which did fucceed.

Cho. Can there be worfe then this is
ftill?

Nun. Yes, this is but a Peccadill.

Cho. Did he for Hawks-meat keep the
Carren?

Or hang 'em up in the next Warren.

Nun. Would it had been as you have said.

No: he insulted o're the dead.

And in a strain most furious,

Spoke thus to each deceased *Puss.*

Butchers are scarce, and dear their Meat:

You'l make a most obleiging Treat.

Delitious Diet, oh how rare!

Then reckons up his *Bill* of *Fare.*

This shall a roasted *Cony* be,

And this shall make a *Fricasee.*

And thou, quoth he, that there dost lye,

Sha't make an excellent *Hare-Pye.*

Briefly, he cook'd 'em: lay'd the Cloath:

Then serv'd them in; but first some broth,

And

And now *Thyestes* (oh sad thought!)
Eats his own Cats, suspecting nought.
Methinks 'tis very dark; I think
I'de best go in and light a Link.

Exit.

Chorus.

Noble *Don John* of *Arles*,
What is it does you thus displease.
What makes you hide behind a Cloud
That pretty Face, as if grown proud?
Has some *Star-Gazer* wrong'd your Fame,
Using, to Vouch a Lye, your Name?
And we who hate their Impudence
Are punisht thus for their Offence?
'Tis a sad thing, and to be pitty'd,
That where a Felony's committed,

K 2　　　　　A

A Jury of *Albumazars*
Find *Billa vera* of the *Stars*;
As *Acceſſarys*, *ſcilicet*
By knowing and concealing it.
Nay ſome there are who in their writing
Pronounce 'em guilty by inciting.
If any miſs a Ring or Spoon
Strait theſe examine Miſtreſs *Moon*,
As Queen of *Nimmers*, or what's worſe,
Executrix of *Moll Cut-Purſe*.
Never was *Bull* ſo bated as is
Taurus by theſe well-willing *Aſſes*.
The *Twins* cannot imbrace in quiet,
Nor do that thing which they don't pry at.
Cancer hath been ſo teaz'd, and took up,
That he ſtarts back if they but look up.
Virgo they ye ſo abus'd, they force her
To looſe her Name, and take a *Coarſer*.

　　　　　　　　　　　For

For who can think her Chaſt, with whom
Men ſo familiar are become?
And in the like abuſive faſhion
They vex each *Star*, and *Conſtellation.*
Leo can't fright 'em from it, no
Nor *Saggitare*, nor *Scorpio*:
But ſtill with their Impertinency's
They fret the *Stars* out of their ſences.
Yet muſt theſe *Almanack Scriblers*
Be to the *Planets* thought Well-willers.
So *Pedagogues* that fle the *Bum*,
In that do the *Boy's* Friends become.

ACT. I.

Atreus Solus.

SO: Now I've taken a Revenge
  Will be as Famous as *Stone-Henge*.
Succeeding Ages will scarce credit
What I have done, when they shall read it:
How kindly I did circumvent,
And treat him in a Punishment;
Yet gin't him too as home and fully
As ever Whore gave Clap to *Bully*.
To feast my Guest with his own Cat,
Is Paramount Revenge, that's flat.
But still to mak't more Tragical,
Thyestes at my feet shall fall;
Dead drunk with double lanted Ale,
In which I le scrape my left Thumb nail.
                   Right!

Right; that will make a charming potion.

See where he comes to meet the motion,

Singing *Old Rofe*, and *Jovial Ca'ches*.

But I'le retire a while; and watch his

Leafure, without like a poor body,

Leaft I difturb the fweet Melody.

Exit.

Enter Thyeftes, *Singing.*

Thyes. *Come lay by your Care, and*—No,

no,

That's not the Key, I am too low.

Try once more —— *Come lay by your Care*

And hang up your forrow —— I there !

What follows? oh —— *Drink on, he's a Sot*

That er'e thinks of to morrow —— What,

Is fore-caft bad ? and is it naught

To drink a health to one's good Thought?

Me-thinks this Song is too too Frolick;
I'le try one that's more Melancholick.

Beneath a Mirtle shade —— But mum;
For now my Tears begin to come.
And whofoever dares engage her,
I'le weep with *Maudlin* for a Wager.

Enter *Atreus*.

Atr. Brother, how is't? *Thy.* Thank ye,
good *Brother*.

Pray how comes all this fmoak & fmother?

Atr. Smoak? where? *Thy.* Why all a-
bout the Room.

Ten Chimny's can't make fuch a Fume,
Look where it rifes at your Feet;
It makes my Eyes run or'e to fee't.

Atr. (*afide.*) See, fee, how the poor
Baby cry's,
Sure 'tis the Ale works through his Eyes.

'Tis

Tis even fo, the fottifh *Drinker*

Is got as Fudled as a *Tinker.*

But that fha'nt ferve: I'le make him er'e

I've done, as drunk as any Bear. ——

Brother, my Wife defires to be

Remember'd to you, and de'e fee;

Has fent you here a merry Wafail,

Which is as good as fhe, or as Ale

Cou'd make. A taft of Love fhe ment it,

And therefore Kift the Cup, and fent it;

You underftand me? *Thy.* Very well.

Thy Wife's an honeft *Doxy-Dell.* ——

Without all doubt, this cunning Gipfy.

afide

Longs for once more, or I am tipfy——

Give me the Bowl — (*drinks*)—— Now tell

 the Quean

All's off; and fhee'l know what I mean.

And

And hark ye. Tell her that I greet her
Kindly, and will not fail to meet her.

Atr. Good. —— *Thy.* Hark ye, Brother,
does your Room

Here, learn to dance? So I presume:

It turns upon the Toe so smoothly,

And quick withall, I tell you soothly,

It makes me giddy with its wheeling!

Motion, and sets me to a Reeling——

Atr. Reeling, that's my Cue. Now I
may

Discover the Intrigue o'th' Play.

Since in that door the Wind is got,

'Tis time to reconcile the Plot. ——

How do you like your Cats my Friend?

Thy. Well; but I dare not much commend

For fear you steal 'em ; nor is this same
Fear vain and Pannique, for I miss 'em.

                              At.

Atr. 'Las they've miscarri'd all to day,

Some hang'd, some drown'd, as one may say

And 'cause they should not basely fall,

'Twas I, dear heart, that kill'd 'em all.

   Thy. Was this done like a loving Brother?

Or like a Friend? Sure neither nother,

But let that pass; I'le spare my Curses——

Their skins will make me three good purses.

I'le goe and flea 'em. *Atr.* But the Jest is

You 'ave dined upon 'em, dear *Thyestes.*

And I both Butcher was, and Cook

To serve you Sir. *Thy.* Now I could puke——

O *Cuckold Cook* to 'Treat me thus !

O hated Hang-dog to hang Puss !

O Son of an old rotten Whore ! |

In *fine*——I'le sleep and tell you more.

Lies down.

Atr.

Atr. Io, *Victoria*! now at laſt

Ey me, and Fortune thou art caſt.

Lye there. Such Victories as theſe are

Will ſwell me up as big as *Cæſar*.

When the *High Germans* he bumbaſted.

Leſs Triumph and content he taſted,

Even now, ſince thus my *Brother* fell,

I ſeem as tall as a High Conſtable.

F I N I S.

EPILOGUE.

Thus, Readers, have ye seen Thyestes Feast,
Both as a History, and a Jest:
The substance and the shaddow of the Play.
No doubt you are great Judges now--Faith say
Which Diet likes ye best, as 'tis before ye?
Or which of these you think the truest Story?
Whether Heroique Fustian drest in Meeter,
Or Mimmick Fare in Jingling Rhime sounds
sweeter?
Which raises most Concern, which most sur-
prise,
No Plot, no Characters, or no Disguise?

Say

Say what you please of Seneca, it is
All one to him whether you Clap or Hiss.
But know, th' applause which Stationers desire
Is not so much to praise a Muse as buy her.
What e're your Authors, or your Actors think,
Your Man of Trade admires not Claps, but
Chink.